COLLINS
WORLD ATLAS

Collins World Atlas

Collins
An Imprint of HarperCollinsPublishers
77-85 Fulham Palace Road
London W6 8JB

First Published 1986
Second Edition 1991
Third Edition 1993
Fourth Edition 1994

Fifth Edition 1997
Reprinted 1998
Revised 1998
Reprinted 1999 (twice)
Reprinted with changes 2000
Reprinted 2000
This edition produced for Remainders Ltd. in 2004
by HarperCollins Publishers.

Copyright ©HarperCollins*Publishers* Ltd 1997
Maps © Bartholomew Ltd 1997

Collins® is a registered trademark of
HarperCollins*Publishers* Ltd

Printed in Spain

ISBN 0 00 763336 X

Cover photo: Zefa Pictures

Visit the booklover's website
www.fireandwater.com

CONTENTS

KU-326-421

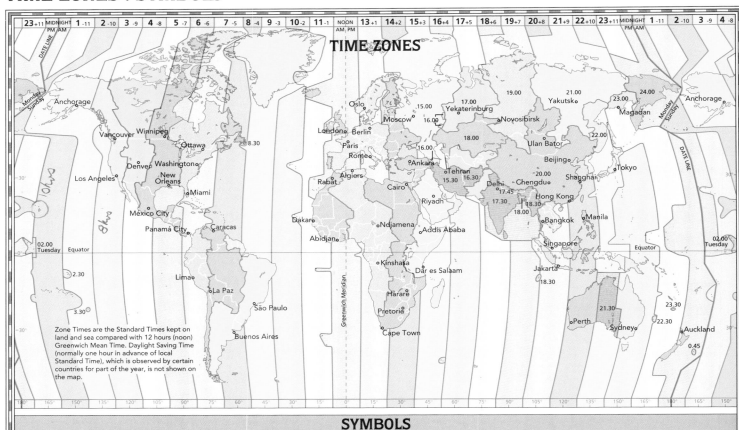

TIME ZONES

Zone Times are the Standard Times kept on land and sea compared with 12 hours (noon) Greenwich Mean Time. Daylight Saving Time (normally one hour in advance of local Standard Time), which is observed by certain countries for part of the year, is not shown on the map.

SYMBOLS

PHYSICAL FEATURES

- Freshwater lake
- Seasonal freshwater lake
- Saltwater lake *or* Lagoon
- Seasonal saltwater lake
- Dry salt lake *or* Salt pan
- Marsh
- River
- Waterfall
- Dam or Barrage
- Seasonal river *or* Wadi
- Canal
- Flood dyke
- Reef
- Volcano
- Lava field
- Sandy desert
- Rocky desert
- Oasis
- Escarpment
- Mountain pass
  height in metres
  923
- Ice cap or Glacier

COMMUNICATIONS

- Motorway
- Motorway tunnel

Motorways are classified separately at scales greater than 1:5 million. At smaller scales motorways are classified with main roads.

- Main road
- Main road under construction
- Main road tunnel
- Other road
- Other road under construction
- Other road tunnel
- Track
- Main railway
- Main railway under construction
- Main railway tunnel
- Other railway
- Other railway under construction
- Other railway tunnel
- ⊕ Main airport
- ⊥ Other airport

RELIEF

METRES	FEET
6000	19686
5000	16409
4000	13124
3000	9843
2000	6562
1000	3281
500	1640
200	656
SEA	LEVEL
200	656
2000	6562
4000	13124
6000	19686

213
△ Summit
height in metres

BOUNDARIES

- International
- International disputed
- Ceasefire line
- Main administrative (U.K.)
- Main administrative
- Main administrative through water

OTHER FEATURES

- National park
- Reserve
- Ancient wall
- ∴ Historic or Tourist site

SETTLEMENTS

POPULATION	NATIONAL CAPITAL	ADMINISTRATIVE CAPITAL	CITY OR TOWN
Over 5 million	▣ **Beijing**	◉ **Tianjin**	◉ **New York**
1 to 5 million	▣ **Seoul**	◉ **Lagos**	◉ **Barranquilla**
500000 to 1 million	▣ **Bangui**	◉ **Douala**	◉ **Memphis**
100000 to 500000	▢ Wellington	○ Mansa	○ Mara
50000 to 100000	▢ Port of Spain	○ Lubango	○ Arecibo
10000 to 50000	▫ Malabo	○ Chinhoyi	○ El Tigre
Less than 10000	▫ Roseau	○ Áti	○ Soledad

Urban area

© 0

COUNTRY	AREA		POPULATION	CAPITAL CITY	MAIN LANGUAGES	MAIN RELIGIONS	CURRENCY
	sq km	sq mls					
EUROPE							
ALBANIA	28 748	11 100	3 645 000	Tirana	Albanian (Gheg, Tosk dialects)	Muslim, Greek Orthodox	Lek
ANDORRA	465	180	68 000	Andorra la Vella	Catalan, Spanish, French	R.C.	French franc, Spanish peseta
AUSTRIA	83 855	32 377	8 053 000	Vienna	German, Croatian, Turkish	R.C., Protestant	Schilling
BELARUS	207 600	80 155	10 141 000	Minsk	Belorussian, Russian, Ukrainian	Belorussian Orthodox, R.C.	Rouble
BELGIUM	30 520	11 784	10 113 000	Brussels	Dutch (Flemish), French, German, Italian	R.C., Protestant	Franc
BOSNIA-HERZEGOVINA	51 130	19 741	4 484 000	Sarajevo	Bosnian, Serbian, Croatia	Muslim, Serbian Orthodox, R.C., Protestant	Dinar
BULGARIA	110 994	42 855	8 402 000	Sofia	Bulgarian, Turkish, Romany, Macedonian	Bulgarian Orthodox, Muslim	Lev
CROATIA	56 538	21 829	4 495 000	Zagreb	Croatian, Serbian	R.C., Orthodox, Muslim	Kuna
CZECH REPUBLIC	78 864	30 450	10 331 000	Prague	Czech, Moravian, Slovak	R.C., Protestant	Koruna
DENMARK	43 075	16 631	5 228 000	Copenhagen	Danish	Protestant, R.C.	Krone
ESTONIA	45 200	17 452	1 530 000	Tallinn	Estonian, Russian	Protestant, Russian Orthodox	Kroon
FINLAND	338 145	130 559	5 108 000	Helsinki	Finnish, Swedish	Protestant, Finnish (Greek) Orthodox	Markka
FRANCE	543 965	210 026	58 143 000	Paris	French, French dialects, Arabic, German (Alsatian), Breton	R.C., Protestant, Muslim	Franc
GERMANY	357 868	138 174	81 642 000	Berlin	German, Turkish	Protestant, R.C., Muslim	Mark
GREECE	131 957	50 949	10 458 000	Athens	Greek, Macedonian	Greek Orthodox, Muslim	Drachma
HUNGARY	93 030	35 919	10 225 000	Budapest	Hungarian, Romany, German, Slovak	R.C., Protestant	Forint
ICELAND	102 820	39 699	269 000	Reykjavik	Icelandic	Protestant, R.C.	Króna
ITALY	301 245	116 311	57 187 000	Rome	Italian, Italian dialects	R.C.	Lira
LATVIA	63 700	24 595	2 515 000	Riga	Latvian, Russian	Protestant, R.C., Russian Orthodox	Lat
LIECHTENSTEIN	160	62	31 000	Vaduz	German	R.C., Protestant	Swiss franc
LITHUANIA	65 200	25 174	3 715 000	Vilnius	Lithuanian, Russian, Polish	R.C., Protestant, Russian Orthodox	Litas
LUXEMBOURG	2 586	998	410 000	Luxembourg	Letzeburgish (Luxembourgian), German, French, Portuguese	R.C., Protestant	Franc
MACEDONIA, Former Yugoslav Republic of	25 713	9 928	2 163 000	Skopje	Macedonian, Albanian, Turkish, Romany	Macedonian Orthodox, Muslim, R.C.	Denar
MALTA	316	122	371 000	Valletta	Maltese, English	R.C.	Lira
MOLDOVA	33 700	13 012	4 432 000	Chişinău	Romanian, Russian, Ukrainian, Gagauz	Moldovan Orthodox, Russian Orthodox	Leu
MONACO	2	1	32 000	Monaco	French, Monegasque, Italian	R.C.	French franc
NETHERLANDS	41 526	16 033	15 451 000	Amsterdam	Dutch, Frisian, Turkish, Indonesian languages	R.C., Protestant, Muslim	Guilder
NORWAY	323 878	125 050	4 360 000	Oslo	Norwegian	Protestant, R.C.	Krone
POLAND	312 683	120 728	38 588 000	Warsaw	Polish, German	R.C., Polish Orthodox	Złoty
PORTUGAL	88 940	34 340	10 797 000	Lisbon	Portuguese	R.C., Protestant	Escudo
REPUBLIC OF IRELAND	70 282	27 136	3 582 000	Dublin	English, Irish	R.C., Protestant	Punt
ROMANIA	237 500	91 699	22 680 000	Bucharest	Romanian, Hungarian	Romanian Orthodox, R.C., Protestant	Leu
RUSSIAN FEDERATION	17 075 400	6 592 849	148 141 000	Moscow	Russian, Tatar, Ukrainian, many local languages	Russian Orthodox, Sunni, Muslim, other Christian, Jewish	Rouble
RUSSIAN FEDERATION in Europe	3 955 800	1 527 334	106 918 000				
SAN MARINO	61	24	25 000	San Marino	Italian	R.C.	Italian lira
SLOVAKIA	49 035	18 933	5 364 000	Bratislava	Slovak, Hungarian, Czech	R.C., Protestant, Orthodox	Koruna
SLOVENIA	20 251	7 819	1 984 000	Ljubljana	Slovene, Serbian, Croatian	R.C., Protestant	Tólar
SPAIN	504 782	194 897	39 210 000	Madrid	Spanish, Catalan, Galician, Basque	R.C.	Peseta
SWEDEN	449 964	173 732	8 831 000	Stockholm	Swedish	Protestant, R.C.	Krona
SWITZERLAND	41 293	15 943	7 040 000	Bern	German, French, Italian, Romansch	R.C., Protestant	Franc
UNITED KINGDOM	244 082	94 241	58 258 000	London	English, South Indian languages, Chinese, Welsh, Gaelic	Protestant, R.C., Muslim, Sikh, Hindu, Jewish	Pound
UKRAINE	603 700	233 090	51 639 000	Kiev	Ukrainian, Russian, regional languages	Ukrainian Orthodox, R.C.	Hryvnia
VATICAN CITY	0.44	0.17	1 000		Italian	R.C.	Italian lira
YUGOSLAVIA	102 173	39 449	10 544 000	Belgrade	Serbian, Albanian, Hungarian	Serbian Orthodox, Montenegrin Orthodox, Muslim	Dinar
ASIA							
AFGHANISTAN	652 225	251 825	20 141 000	Kabul	Dari, Pushtu, Uzbek, Turkmen	Muslim	Afghani
ARMENIA	29 800	11 506	3 599 000	Yerevan	Armenian, Azeri, Russian	Arm. Orthodox, R.C., Muslim	Dram
AZERBAIJAN	86 600	33 436	7 499 000	Baku	Azeri, Armenian, Russian, Lezgian	Muslim, Russian and Armenian Orthodox	Manat
BAHRAIN	691	267	586 000	Manama	Arabic, English	Muslim, Christian	Dinar
BANGLADESH	143 998	55 598	120 433 000	Dhaka	Bengali, Bihari, Hindi, English, local languages	Muslim, Hindu, Buddhist, Christian	Taka
BHUTAN	46 620	18 000	1 638 000	Thimphu	Dzongkha, Nepali, Assamese, English	Buddhist, Hindu, Muslim	Ngultrum, Indian rupee
BRUNEI	5 765	2 226	285 000	Bandar Seri Begawan	Malay, English, Chinese	Muslim, Buddhist, Christian	Dollar (Ringgit)
CAMBODIA	181 000	69 884	9 836 000	Phnom Penh	Khmer, Vietnamese	Buddhist, R.C., Muslim	Riel
CHINA	9 560 900	3 691 484	1 221 462 000	Beijing	Chinese, regional languages	Confucian, Taoist, Buddhist, Muslim, R.C.	Yuan
CYPRUS	9 251	3 572	742 000	Nicosia	Greek, Turkish, English	Greek Orthodox, Muslim	Pound
EAST TIMOR	14 874	5 743	857 000	Dili	Portuguese, Tetun, English	Roman Catholic	Rupiah
GEORGIA	69 700	26 911	5 457 000	Tbilisi	Georgian, Russian, Armenian, Azeri, Ossetian, Abkhaz	Georgian & Russian Orthodox, Muslim	Lari
INDIA	3 287 263	1 269 219	935 744 000	New Delhi	Hindi, English, regional languages	Hindu, Muslim, Sikh, Christian, Buddhist, Jain	Rupee
INDONESIA	1 919 445	741 102	194 564 000	Jakarta	Indonesian, local languages	Muslim, Protestant, R.C. Hindu, Buddhist	Rupiah
IRAN	1 648 000	636 296	67 283 000	Tehran	Farsi, Azeri, Kurdish, regional languages	Muslim, Baha'i, Christian, Zoroastrian	Rial
IRAQ	438 317	169 235	20 449 000	Baghdad	Arabic, Kurdish, Turkmen	Muslim, R.C.	Dinar
ISRAEL	20 770	8 019	5 545 000	Jerusalem	Hebrew, Arabic, Yiddish, English	Jewish, Muslim, Christian, Druze	Shekel
JAPAN	377 727	145 841	125 197 000	Tokyo	Japanese	Shintoist, Buddhist, Christian	Yen
JORDAN	89 206	34 443	5 439 000	Amman	Arabic	Muslim, Christian	Dinar

© Collins

4 NATIONAL STATISTICS

COUNTRY	AREA sq km	sq mls	POPULATION	CAPITAL CITY	MAIN LANGUAGES	MAIN RELIGIONS	CURRENCY
KAZAKSTAN	2 717 300	1 049 155	16 590 000	Astana	Kazakh, Russian, German, Ukrainian, Uzbek, Tatar	Muslim, Russian. Orthodox, Protestant	Tanga
KUWAIT	17 818	6 880	1 691 000	Kuwait	Arabic	Muslim, Christian, Hindu	Dinar
KYRGYZSTAN	198 500	76 641	4 668 000	Bishkek	Kirghiz, Russian, Uzbek	Muslim, Russian Orthodox	Som
LAOS	236 800	91 429	4 882 000	Vientiane	Lao, local languages	Buddhist, trad. beliefs, R.C., Muslim	Kip
LEBANON	10 452	4 036	3 009 000	Beirut	Arabic, French, Armenian	Muslim, Protestant, R.C.	Pound
MALAYSIA	332 965	128 559	20 140 000	Kuala Lumpur	Malay, English, Chinese, Tamil, local languages	Muslim, Buddhist, Hindu, Christian, trad. beliefs	Dollar (Ringgit)
MALDIVES	298	115	254 000	Male	Divehi (Maldivian)	Muslim	Rufiyaa
MONGOLIA	1 565 000	604 250	2 410 000	Ulan Bator	Khalka (Mongolian), Kazakh, local languages	Buddhist, Muslim, trad. beliefs	Tugrik
MYANMAR	676 577	261 228	46 527 000	Yangon	Burmese, Shan, Karen, local languages	Buddhist, Muslim, Protestant, R.C.	Kyat
NEPAL	147 181	56 827	21 918 000	Kathmandu	Nepali, Maithili, Bhojpuri, English, local languages	Hindu, Buddhist, Muslim	Rupee
NORTH KOREA	120 538	46 540	23 917 000	Pyongyang	Korean	Trad. beliefs, Chondoist, Buddhist, Confucian, Taoist	Won
OMAN	271 950	105 000	2 163 000	Muscat	Arabic, Baluchi, Farsi, Swahili, Indian languages	Muslim	Rial
PAKISTAN	803 940	310 403	129 808 000	Islamabad	Urdu, Punjabi, Sindhi, Pushtu, English	Muslim, Christian, Hindu	Rupee
PALAU	497	192	17 000	Koror	Palauan, English	R.C., Protestant, trad.beliefs	US dollar
PHILIPPINES	300 000	115 831	70 267 000	Manila	English, Filipino, Cebuano, local languages	R.C., Aglipayan, Muslim, Protestant	Peso
QATAR	11 437	4 416	551 000	Doha	Arabic, Indian languages	Muslim, Christian, Hindu	Riyal
RUSSIAN FEDERATION	17 075 400	6 592 849	148 141 000	Moscow	Russian, Tatar, Ukrainian, local languages	Russian Orthodox, Muslim, other Christian, Jewish	Rouble
RUSSIAN FEDERATION in Asia	13 119 600	5 065 478	41 223 000				
SAUDI ARABIA	2 200 000	849 425	17 880 000	Riyadh	Arabic	Muslim	Riyal
SINGAPORE	639	247	2 987 000	Singapore	Chinese, English, Malay, Tamil	Buddhist, Taoist, Muslim, Christian, Hindu	Dollar
SOUTH KOREA	99 274	38 330	44 851 000	Seoul	Korean	Buddhist, Protestant, R.C., Confucian, trad. beliefs	Won
SRI LANKA	65 610	25 332	18 354 000	Colombo	Sinhalese, Tamil, English	Buddhist, Hindu, Muslim, R.C.	Rupee
SYRIA	185 180	71 498	14 186 000	Damascus	Arabic, Kurdish, Armenian	Muslim, Christian	Pound
TAIWAN	36 179	13 969	21 211 000	Taipei	Chinese, local languages	Buddhist, Taoist, Confucian, Christian	Dollar
TAJIKISTAN	143 100	55 251	5 836 000	Dushanbe	Tajik, Uzbek, Russian	Muslim	Rouble
THAILAND	513 115	198 115	59 401 000	Bangkok	Thai, Lao, Chinese, Malay, Mon-Khmer languages	Buddhist, Muslim	Baht
TURKEY	779 452	300 948	61 644 000	Ankara	Turkish, Kurdish	Muslim	Lira
TURKMENISTAN	488 100	188 456	4 099 000	Ashkhabad	Turkmen, Russian	Muslim	Manat
UNITED ARAB EMIRATES	77 700	30 000	2 314 000	Abu Dhabi	Arabic, English, Hindi, Urdu, Farsi	Muslim, Christian	Dirham
UZBEKISTAN	447 400	172 742	22 843 000	Tashkent	Uzbek, Russian, Tajik, Kazakh	Muslim, Russian Orthodox	Som
VIETNAM	329 565	127 246	74 545 000	Hanoi	Vietnamese, Thai, Khmer, Chinese, local languages	Buddhist, Taoist, R.C., Cao Dai, Hoa Hao	Dong
YEMEN	527 968	203 850	14 501 000	Sana	Arabic	Muslim	Dinar, Rial

OCEANIA

COUNTRY	AREA sq km	sq mls	POPULATION	CAPITAL CITY	MAIN LANGUAGES	MAIN RELIGIONS	CURRENCY
AUSTRALIA	7 682 300	2 966 136	18 054 000	Canberra	English, Italian, Greek, Aboriginal languages	Protestant, R.C., Orthodox, Aboriginal beliefs	Dollar
FIJI	18 330	7 077	784 000	Suva	English, Fijian, Hindi	Protestant, Hindu, R.C., Muslim	Dollar
KIRIBATI	717	277	79 000	Bairiki	I-Kiribati (Gilbertese), English	R.C., Protestant, Baha'i, Mormon	Austr. dollar
MARSHALL ISLANDS	181	70	56 000	Dalap-Uliga-Darrit	Marshallese, English	Protestant, R.C.	US dollar
FED. STATES OF MICRONESIA	701	271	105 000	Palikir	English, Trukese, Pohnpeian, local languages	Protestant, R.C.	US dollar
NAURU	21	8	11 000	Yaren	Nauruan, Gilbertese, English	Protestant, R.C.	Austr. dollar
NEW ZEALAND	270 534	104 454	3 542 000	Wellington	English, Maori	Protestant, R.C.	Dollar
PAPUA NEW GUINEA	462 840	178 704	4 074 000	Port Moresby	English, Tok Pisin, local languages	Protestant, R.C., trad. beliefs	Kina
SAMOA	2 831	1 093	171 000	Apia	Samoan, English	Protestant, R.C., Mormon	Tala
SOLOMON ISLANDS	28 370	10 954	378 000	Honiara	English, Solomon Islands Pidgin, local languages	Protestant, R.C.	Dollar
TONGA	748	289	98 000	Nuku'alofa	Tongan, English	Protestant, R.C., Mormon	Pa'anga
TUVALU	25	10	10 000	Fongafale	Tuvaluan, English	Protestant	Dollar
VANUATU	12 190	4 707	169 000	Port-Vila	English, Bislama, French	Protestant, R.C., trad. beliefs	Vatu

NORTH AMERICA

COUNTRY	AREA sq km	sq mls	POPULATION	CAPITAL CITY	MAIN LANGUAGES	MAIN RELIGIONS	CURRENCY
ANTIGUA & BARBUDA	442	171	66 000	St John's	English, Creole	Protestant, R.C.	E. Carib. dollar
THE BAHAMAS	13 939	5 382	278 000	Nassau	English, Creole, French Creole	Protestant, R.C.	Dollar
BARBADOS	430	166	264 000	Bridgetown	English, Creole (Bajan)	Protestant, R.C.	Dollar
BELIZE	22 965	8 867	217 000	Belmopan	English, Creole, Spanish, Mayan	R.C., Protestant, Hindu	Dollar
CANADA	9 970 610	3 849 653	29 606 000	Ottawa	English, French, Amerindian languages, Inuktitut (Eskimo)	R.C., Protestant, Greek Orthodox, Jewish	Dollar
COSTA RICA	51 100	19 730	3 333 000	San José	Spanish	R.C., Protestant	Colón
CUBA	110 860	42 803	11 041 000	Havana	Spanish	R.C., Protestant	Peso
DOMINICA	750	290	71 000	Roseau	English, French Creole	R.C., Protestant	E. Carib. dollar, Pound, Franc
DOMINICAN REPUBLIC	48 442	18 704	7 915 000	Santo Domingo	Spanish, French Creole	R.C., Protestant	Peso
EL SALVADOR	21 041	8 124	5 768 000	San Salvador	Spanish	R.C., Protestant	Colón
GRENADA	378	146	92 000	St George's	English, Creole	R.C., Protestant	E. Carib. dollar
GUATEMALA	108 890	42 043	10 621 000	Guatemala City	Spanish, Mayan languages	R.C., Protestant	Quetzal
HAITI	27 750	10 714	7 180 000	Port-au-Prince	French, French Creole	R.C., Protestant, Voodoo	Gourde
HONDURAS	112 088	43 277	5 953 000	Tegucigalpa	Spanish, Amerindian languages	R.C., Protestant	Lempira
JAMAICA	10 991	4 244	2 530 000	Kingston	English, Creole	Protestant, R.C., Rastafarian	Dollar
MEXICO	1 972 545	761 604	90 487 000	Mexico City	Spanish, Amerindian languages	R.C., Protestant	Peso
NICARAGUA	130 000	50 193	4 539 000	Managua	Spanish, Amerindian languages	R.C., Protestant	Córdoba
PANAMA	77 082	29 762	2 631 000	Panama City	Spanish, English Creole, Amerindian languages	R.C., Protestant, Muslim, Baha'i	Balboa
ST KITTS-NEVIS	261	101	42 000	Basseterre	English, Creole	Protestant, R.C.	E. Carib. dollar
ST LUCIA	616	238	145 000	Castries	English, French Creole	R.C., Protestant	E. Carib. dollar
ST VINCENT & THE GRENADINES	389	150	111 000	Kingstown	English, Creole	Protestant, R.C.	E. Carib. dollar
TRINIDAD AND TOBAGO	5 130	1 981	1 306 000	Port of Spain	English, Creole, Hindi	R.C., Hindu, Protestant, Muslim	Dollar
USA	9 809 386	3 787 425	263 034 000	Washington	English, Spanish, Amerindian languages	Protestant, R.C., Muslim, Jewish, Mormon	Dollar

COUNTRY	AREA		POPULATION	CAPITAL CITY	MAIN LANGUAGES	MAIN RELIGIONS	CURRENCY
	sq km	sq mls					
SOUTH AMERICA							
ARGENTINA	2 766 889	1 068 302	34 768 000	Buenos Aires	Spanish, Italian, Amerindian languages	R.C., Protestant, Jewish	Peso
BOLIVIA	1 098 581	424 164	7 414 000	La Paz	Spanish, Quechua, Aymara	R.C., Protestant, Baha'i	Boliviano
BRAZIL	8 511 965	3 286 470	155 822 000	Brasília	Portuguese, German, Japanese, Italian, Amerindian languages	R.C., Spiritist, Protestant	Real
CHILE	756 945	292 258	14 210 000	Santiago	Spanish, Amerindian languages	R.C., Protestant	Peso
COLOMBIA	1 141 748	440 831	35 099 000	Bogotá	Spanish, Amerindian languages	R.C., Protestant	Peso
ECUADOR	272 045	105 037	11 460 000	Quito	Spanish, Quechua, Amerind. lang.	R.C., Protestant	Sucre
FRENCH GUIANA	90 000	34 749	147 000	Cayenne	French, French Creole	R.C., Protestant	French franc
GUYANA	214 969	83 000	835 000	Georgetown	English, Creole, Hindi, Amerindian languages	Protestant, Hindu, R.C., Muslim	Dollar
PARAGUAY	406 752	157 048	4 828 000	Asunción	Spanish, Guaraní	R.C., Protestant	Guaraní
PERU	1 285 216	496 225	23 560 000	Lima	Spanish, Quechua, Aymara	R.C., Protestant	Sol
SURINAME	163 820	63 251	423 000	Paramaribo	Dutch, Surinamese, English, Hindi, Javanese	Hindu, R.C., Protestant, Muslim	Guilder
URUGUAY	176 215	68 037	3 186 000	Montevideo	Spanish	R.C., Protestant, Jewish	Peso
VENEZUELA	912 050	352 144	21 644 000	Caracas	Spanish, Amerindian languages	R.C., Protestant	Bolívar
AFRICA							
ALGERIA	2 381 741	919 595	28 548 000	Algiers	Arabic, French, Berber	Muslim, R.C.	Dinar
ANGOLA	1 246 700	481 354	11 072 000	Luanda	Portuguese, local languages	R.C., Protestant, trad. beliefs	Kwanza
BENIN	112 620	43 483	5 561 000	Porto Novo	French, Fon, Yoruba, Adja, local languages	Trad. beliefs, R.C., Muslim	CFA franc
BOTSWANA	581 370	224 468	1 456 000	Gaborone	English, Setswana, Shona, local languages	Trad. beliefs, Protestant, R.C.	Pula
BURKINA	274 200	105 869	10 200 000	Ouagadougou	French, More (Mossi), Fulani, local languages	Trad. beliefs, Muslim, R.C.	CFA franc
BURUNDI	27 835	10 747	5 982 000	Bujumbura	Kirundi (Hutu, Tutsi), French	R.C., trad. beliefs, Protestant, Muslim	Franc
CAMEROON	475 442	183 569	13 277 000	Yaoundé	French, English, Fang, Bamileke, local languages	Trad. beliefs, R.C., Muslim, Protestant	CFA franc
CAPE VERDE	4 033	1 557	392 000	Praia	Portuguese, Portuguese Creole	R.C., Protestant, trad. beliefs	Escudo
C. A. R.	622 436	240 324	3 315 000	Bangui	French, Sango, Banda, Baya, local languages	Protestant, R.C., trad. beliefs, Muslim	CFA franc
CHAD	1 284 000	495 755	6 361 000	Ndjamena	Arabic, French, local languages	Muslim, trad. beliefs, R.C.	CFA franc
COMOROS	1 862	719	653 000	Moroni	Comorian, French, Arabic	Muslim, R.C.	Franc
CONGO	342 000	132 047	2 590 000	Brazzaville	French, Kongo, Monokutuba, local languages	R.C., Protestant, trad. beliefs, Muslim	CFA franc
CONGO, DEM. REP.	2 345 410	905 568	43 901 000	Kinshasa	French, Lingala, Swahili, Kongo, local languages	R.C., Protestant, Muslim, trad. beliefs	Franc
CÔTE D'IVOIRE	322 463	124 504	14 230 000	Yamoussoukro	French, Akan, local languages	Trad. beliefs, Muslim, R.C.	CFA franc
DJIBOUTI	23 200	8 958	577 000	Djibouti	Somali, French, Arabic, Issa, Afar	Muslim, R.C.	Franc
EGYPT	1 000 250	386 199	59 226 000	Cairo	Arabic, French	Muslim, Coptic Christian	Pound
EQUATORIAL GUINEA	28 051	10 831	400 000	Malabo	Spanish, Fang	R.C., trad. beliefs	CFA franc
ERITREA	117 400	45 328	3 531 000	Asmara	Tigrinya, Arabic, Tigre, English	Muslim, Coptic Christian	Ethiopian birr
ETHIOPIA	1 133 880	437 794	56 677 000	Addis Ababa	Amharic, Oromo, local languages	Ethiopian Orthodox, Muslim, trad. beliefs	Birr
GABON	267 667	103 347	1 320 000	Libreville	French, Fang, local languages	R.C., Protestant, trad. beliefs	CFA franc
GAMBIA	11 295	4 361	1 118 000	Banjul	English, Malinke, Fulani, Wolof	Muslim, Protestant	Dalasi
GHANA	238 537	92 100	17 453 000	Accra	English, Hausa, Akan, local languages	Protestant, R.C., Muslim, trad. beliefs	Cedi
GUINEA	245 857	94 926	6 700 000	Conakry	French, Fulani, local languages	Muslim, trad. beliefs, R.C.	Franc
GUINEA-BISSAU	36 125	13 948	1 073 000	Bissau	Portuguese, Portuguese Creole, local languages	Trad. beliefs, Muslim, R.C.	Peso
KENYA	582 646	224 961	30 522 000	Nairobi	Swahili, English, local languages	R.C., Protestant, trad. beliefs	Shilling
LESOTHO	30 355	11 720	2 050 000	Maseru	Sesotho, English, Zulu	R.C., Protestant, trad. beliefs	Loti
LIBERIA	111 369	43 000	2 760 000	Monrovia	English, Creole, local languages	Trad. beliefs, Muslim, Protestant, R.C.	Dollar
LIBYA	1 759 540	679 362	5 407 000	Tripoli	Arabic, Berber	Muslim, R.C.	Dinar
MADAGASCAR	587 041	226 658	14 763 000	Antananarivo	Malagasy, French	Trad. beliefs, R.C., Protestant, Muslim	Franc
MALAWI	118 484	45 747	9 788 000	Lilongwe	English, Chichewa, Lomwe, local languages	Protestant, R.C., trad. beliefs, Muslim	Kwacha
MALI	1 240 140	478 821	10 795 000	Bamako	French, Bambara, local languages	Muslim, trad. beliefs, R.C.	CFA franc
MAURITANIA	1 030 700	397 955	2 284 000	Nouakchott	Arabic, French, local languages	Muslim	Ouguiya
MAURITIUS	2 040	788	1 122 000	Port Louis	English, French Creole, Hindi, Indian languages	Hindu, R.C., Muslim, Protestant	Rupee
MOROCCO	446 550	172 414	27 111 000	Rabat	Arabic, Berber, French, Spanish	Muslim, R.C.	Dirham
MOZAMBIQUE	799 380	308 642	17 423 000	Maputo	Portuguese, Makua, Tsonga, local languages	Trad. beliefs, R.C., Muslim	Metical
NAMIBIA	824 292	318 261	1 540 000	Windhoek	English, Afrikaans, German, Ovambo, local languages	Protestant, R.C.	Dollar
NIGER	1 267 000	489 191	9 151 000	Niamey	French, Hausa, local languages	Muslim, trad. beliefs	CFA franc
NIGERIA	923 768	356 669	111 721 000	Abuja	English, Creole, Hausa, Yoruba, Ibo, Fulani	Muslim, Protestant, R.C., trad. beliefs	Naira
RWANDA	26 338	10 169	7 952 000	Kigali	Kinyarwanda, French, English	R.C., trad. beliefs, Protestant, Muslim	Franc
SAO TOME AND PRINCIPE	964	372	127 000	São Tomé	Portuguese, Portuguese Creole	R.C., Protestant	Dobra
SENEGAL	196 720	75 954	8 347 000	Dakar	French, Wolof, local languages	Muslim, R.C., trad. beliefs	CFA franc
SEYCHELLES	455	176	75 000	Victoria	Seychellois, English	R.C., Protestant	Rupee
SIERRA LEONE	71 740	27 699	4 509 000	Freetown	English, Creole, Mende, Temne, local languages	Trad. beliefs, Muslim, Protestant, R.C.	Leone
SOMALIA	637 657	246 201	9 250 000	Mogadishu	Somali, Arabic	Muslim	Shilling
SOUTH AFRICA	1 219 080	470 689	41 244 000	Pretoria/ Cape Town	Afrikaans, English, local languages	Protestant, R.C., Muslim, Hindu	Rand
SUDAN	2 505 813	967 494	28 098 000	Khartoum	Arabic, Dinka, Nubian, Beja, Nuer, local languages	Muslim, trad. beliefs, R.C., Protestant	Dinar
SWAZILAND	17 364	6 704	908 000	Mbabane	Swazi, English	Protestant, R.C., trad. beliefs	Emalangeni
TANZANIA	945 087	364 900	30 337 000	Dodoma	Swahili, English, Nyamwezi, local languages	R.C., Muslim, trad. beliefs, Protestant	Shilling
TOGO	56 785	21 925	4 138 000	Lomé	French, Ewe, Kabre, local languages	Trad. beliefs, R.C., Muslim, Protestant	CFA franc
TUNISIA	164 150	63 379	8 896 000	Tunis	Arabic, French	Muslim	Dinar
UGANDA	241 038	93 065	19 848 000	Kampala	English, Swahili, Luganda, local languages	R.C., Protestant, Muslim, trad. beliefs	Shilling
ZAMBIA	752 614	290 586	9 373 000	Lusaka	English, Bemba, Nyanja, Tonga, local languages	Protestant, R.C., trad. beliefs, Muslim	Kwacha
ZIMBABWE	390 759	150 873	11 526 000	Harare	English, Shona, Ndebele	Protestant, R.C., trad. beliefs	Dollar

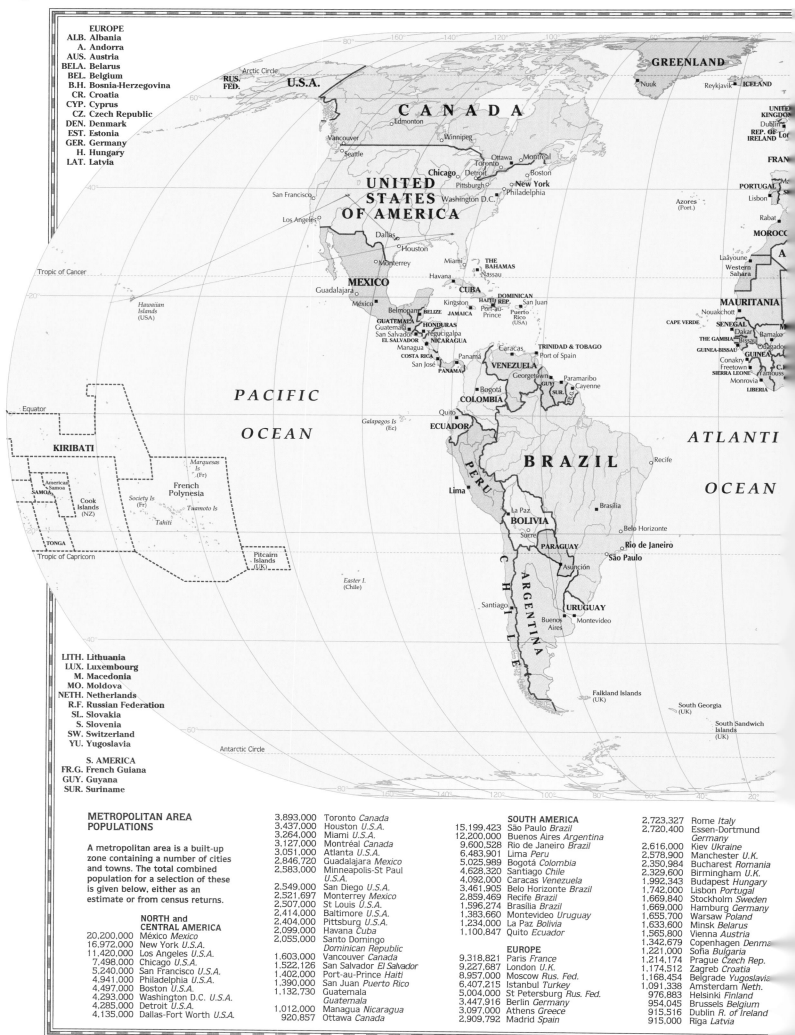

EUROPE
ALB. Albania
A. Andorra
AUS. Austria
BELA. Belarus
BEL. Belgium
B.H. Bosnia-Herzegovina
CR. Croatia
CYP. Cyprus
CZ. Czech Republic
DEN. Denmark
EST. Estonia
GER. Germany
H. Hungary
LAT. Latvia

LITH. Lithuania
LUX. Luxembourg
M. Macedonia
MO. Moldova
NETH. Netherlands
R.F. Russian Federation
SL. Slovakia
S. Slovenia
SW. Switzerland
YU. Yugoslavia

S. AMERICA
FR.G. French Guiana
GUY. Guyana
SUR. Suriname

METROPOLITAN AREA POPULATIONS

A metropolitan area is a built-up zone containing a number of cities and towns. The total combined population for a selection of these is given below, either as an estimate or from census returns.

NORTH and CENTRAL AMERICA

20,200,000	México *Mexico*
16,972,000	New York *U.S.A.*
11,420,000	Los Angeles *U.S.A.*
7,498,000	Chicago *U.S.A.*
5,240,000	San Francisco *U.S.A.*
4,941,000	Philadelphia *U.S.A.*
4,497,000	Boston *U.S.A.*
4,293,000	Washington D.C. *U.S.A.*
4,285,000	Detroit *U.S.A.*
4,135,000	Dallas-Fort Worth *U.S.A.*
3,893,000	Toronto *Canada*
3,437,000	Houston *U.S.A.*
3,264,000	Miami *U.S.A.*
3,127,000	Montréal *Canada*
3,051,000	Atlanta *U.S.A.*
2,846,720	Guadalajara *Mexico*
2,583,000	Minneapolis-St Paul *U.S.A.*
2,549,000	San Diego *U.S.A.*
2,521,697	Monterrey *Mexico*
2,507,000	St Louis *U.S.A.*
2,414,000	Baltimore *U.S.A.*
2,404,000	Pittsburg *U.S.A.*
2,099,000	Havana *Cuba*
2,055,000	Santo Domingo *Dominican Republic*
1,603,000	Vancouver *Canada*
1,522,126	San Salvador *El Salvador*
1,402,000	Port-au-Prince *Haiti*
1,390,000	San Juan *Puerto Rico*
1,132,730	Guatemala *Guatemala*
1,012,000	Managua *Nicaragua*
920,857	Ottawa *Canada*

SOUTH AMERICA

15,199,423	São Paulo *Brazil*
12,200,000	Buenos Aires *Argentina*
9,600,528	Rio de Janeiro *Brazil*
6,483,901	Lima *Peru*
5,025,989	Bogotá *Colombia*
4,628,320	Santiago *Chile*
4,092,000	Caracas *Venezuela*
3,461,905	Belo Horizonte *Brazil*
2,859,469	Recife *Brazil*
1,596,274	Brasília *Brazil*
1,383,660	Montevideo *Uruguay*
1,234,000	La Paz *Bolivia*
1,100,847	Quito *Ecuador*

EUROPE

9,318,821	Paris *France*
9,227,687	London *U.K.*
8,957,000	Moscow *Rus. Fed.*
6,407,215	Istanbul *Turkey*
5,004,000	St Petersburg *Rus. Fed.*
3,447,916	Berlin *Germany*
3,097,000	Athens *Greece*
2,909,792	Madrid *Spain*
2,723,327	Rome *Italy*
2,720,400	Essen-Dortmund *Germany*
2,616,000	Kiev *Ukraine*
2,578,900	Manchester *U.K.*
2,350,984	Bucharest *Romania*
2,329,600	Birmingham *U.K.*
1,992,343	Budapest *Hungary*
1,742,000	Lisbon *Portugal*
1,669,840	Stockholm *Sweden*
1,669,000	Hamburg *Germany*
1,655,700	Warsaw *Poland*
1,633,600	Minsk *Belarus*
1,565,800	Vienna *Austria*
1,342,679	Copenhagen *Denmark*
1,221,000	Sofia *Bulgaria*
1,214,174	Prague *Czech Rep.*
1,174,512	Zagreb *Croatia*
1,168,454	Belgrade *Yugoslavia*
1,091,338	Amsterdam *Neth.*
976,883	Helsinki *Finland*
954,045	Brussels *Belgium*
915,516	Dublin *R. of Ireland*
915,000	Rīga *Latvia*

1:80M

758,949	Oslo *Norway*
582,000	Vilnius *Lithuania*
499,183	Tallinn *Estonia*
	ASIA
341,896	Shanghai *China*
571,720	Bombay *India*
609,735	Tōkyō *Japan*
916,272	Calcutta *India*
819,407	Beijing *China*
627,000	Seoul *S. Korea*
371,000	Tianjin *China*
253,000	Jakarta *Indonesia*
520,000	Ōsaka-Kōbe *Japan*
375,188	Delhi *India*
832,000	Manila-Quezon City *Philippines*
702,000	Karachi *Pakistan*
773,000	Tehrān *Iran*
105,160	Dhaka *Bangladesh*
376,000	Bangkok *Thailand*
448,000	Hong Kong *China*
361,468	Madras *India*
763,000	Shenyang *China*

4,280,261	Hyderabad *India*
4,092,000	Lahore *Pakistan*
4,086,548	Bangalore *India*
4,044,000	Baghdād *Iraq*
3,924,435	Hồ Chi Minh *Vietnam*
3,921,000	Wuhan *China*
3,797,566	Pusan *S. Korea*
3,671,000	Guangzhou *China*
3,297,655	Ahmadabad *India*
3,295,000	Yangon *Myanmar*
3,250,548	Yokohama *Japan*
3,151,000	Chongqing *China*
3,022,236	Ankara *Turkey*
3,004,000	Chengdu *China*
2,966,000	Harbin *China*
2,913,000	Damascus *Syria*
2,874,000	Singapore *Singapore*
2,859,000	Xi'an *China*
2,768,000	Aleppo *Syria*
2,720,000	T'ai-pei *Taiwan*
2,665,105	Izmir *Turkey*
2,543,000	Dalian *China*
2,485,014	Pune *India*
2,473,272	Surabaya *Indonesia*

2,265,000	Nanjing *China*
2,230,000	P'yŏngyang *N. Korea*
2,214,000	Changchun *China*
2,094,000	Tashkent *Uzbekistan*
2,000,000	Kābul *Afghanistan*
1,711,000	Kuala Lumpur *Malaysia*
1,500,000	Beirut *Lebanon*
1,500,000	Riyadh *Saudi Arabia*
1,442,000	Novosibirsk *Rus. Fed.*
1,400,000	Tbilisi *Georgia*
1,272,000	'Ammān *Jordan*
1,200,000	Yerevan *Armenia*
1,151,300	Almaty *Kazakhstan*
1,056,146	Ha Nôi *Vietnam*
616,000	Colombo *Sri Lanka*
549,900	Jerusalem *Israel*
537,000	Islamabad *Pakistan*
200,000	Kuwait *Kuwait*
	AFRICA
11,642,000	Cairo *Egypt*
5,689,000	Lagos *Nigeria*
3,505,000	Kinshasa *Congo, Dem. Rep.*
3,380,000	Alexandria *Egypt*

3,210,000	Casablanca *Morocco*
3,033,000	Algiers *Algeria*
2,350,157	Cape Town *S. Africa*
1,947,000	Khartoum *Sudan*
1,891,000	Addis Ababa *Ethiopia*
1,717,000	Luanda *Angola*
1,636,000	Tunis *Tunisia*
1,503,000	Nairobi *Kenya*
1,500,000	Tripoli *Libya*
1,492,000	Dakar *Senegal*
1,472,000	Rabat *Morocco*
1,098,000	Maputo *Mozambique*
1,000,000	Harare *Zimbabwe*
523,900	Abuja *Nigeria*
	OCEANIA
3,700,000	Sydney *Australia*
3,178,000	Melbourne *Australia*
1,386,000	Brisbane *Australia*
1,215,000	Perth *Australia*
1,065,000	Adelaide *Australia*
896,200	Auckland *New Zealand*
325,700	Wellington *New Zealand*
310,000	Canberra *Australia*

KM MILES
4000 — 2400
3200
2400 — 1600
1600 — 800
800
0

© Collins

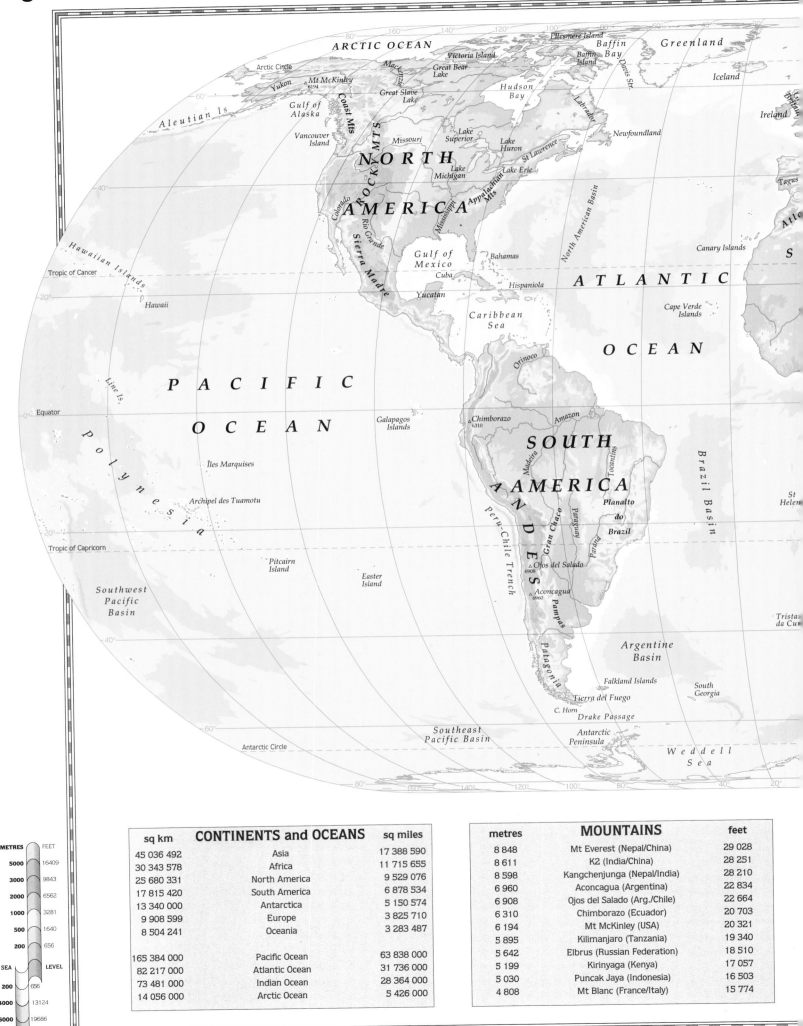

ARCTIC OCEAN · Ellesmere Island · Baffin Bay · Greenland · Victoria Island · Baffin Island · Davis Str. · Iceland · Arctic Circle · Mackenzie · Great Bear Lake · Great Slave Lake · Hudson Bay · Labrador · Ireland · Yukon · Mt McKinley 6194 · Gulf of Alaska · Coast Mts · Newfoundland · Aleutian Is · Vancouver Island · Missouri · Lake Superior · Lake Huron · St Lawrence · Tagus · NORTH AMERICA · ROCKY MTS · Lake Michigan · Lake Erie · Appalachian Mts · Mississippi · North American Basin · Atl · Hawaiian Islands · Colorado · Rio Grande · Sierra Madre · S · Tropic of Cancer · Gulf of Mexico · Bahamas · Canary Islands · Hawaii · Cuba · Hispaniola · ATLANTIC · Yucatan · Caribbean Sea · Cape Verde Islands · Line Is · PACIFIC · Orinoco · OCEAN · Equator · Galapagos Islands · Chimborazo 6310 · Amazon · OCEAN · SOUTH · Madeira · Tocantins · Brazil Basin · St Helena · Polynesia · Îles Marquises · ANDES · AMERICA · Planalto do Brazil · Archipel des Tuamotu · Peru-Chile Trench · Gran Chaco · Paraguay · Paraná · Tropic of Capricorn · Pitcairn Island · Easter Island · Ojos del Salado 6908 · Aconcagua 6960 · Pampas · Tristan da Cu · Southwest Pacific Basin · Argentine Basin · Patagonia · Falkland Islands · South Georgia · Tierra del Fuego · C. Horn · Drake Passage · Southeast Pacific Basin · Antarctic Peninsula · Weddell Sea · Antarctic Circle

Eckert IV Projection

METRES	FEET
5000	16409
3000	9843
2000	6562
1000	3281
500	1640
200	656
SEA	LEVEL
200	656
4000	13124
6000	19686

sq km	CONTINENTS and OCEANS	sq miles
45 036 492	Asia	17 388 590
30 343 578	Africa	11 715 655
25 680 331	North America	9 529 076
17 815 420	South America	6 878 534
13 340 000	Antarctica	5 150 574
9 908 599	Europe	3 825 710
8 504 241	Oceania	3 283 487
165 384 000	Pacific Ocean	63 838 000
82 217 000	Atlantic Ocean	31 736 000
73 481 000	Indian Ocean	28 364 000
14 056 000	Arctic Ocean	5 426 000

metres	MOUNTAINS	feet
8 848	Mt Everest (Nepal/China)	29 028
8 611	K2 (India/China)	28 251
8 598	Kangchenjunga (Nepal/India)	28 210
6 960	Aconcagua (Argentina)	22 834
6 908	Ojos del Salado (Arg./Chile)	22 664
6 310	Chimborazo (Ecuador)	20 703
6 194	Mt McKinley (USA)	20 321
5 895	Kilimanjaro (Tanzania)	19 340
5 642	Elbrus (Russian Federation)	18 510
5 199	Kirinyaga (Kenya)	17 057
5 030	Puncak Jaya (Indonesia)	16 503
4 808	Mt Blanc (France/Italy)	15 774

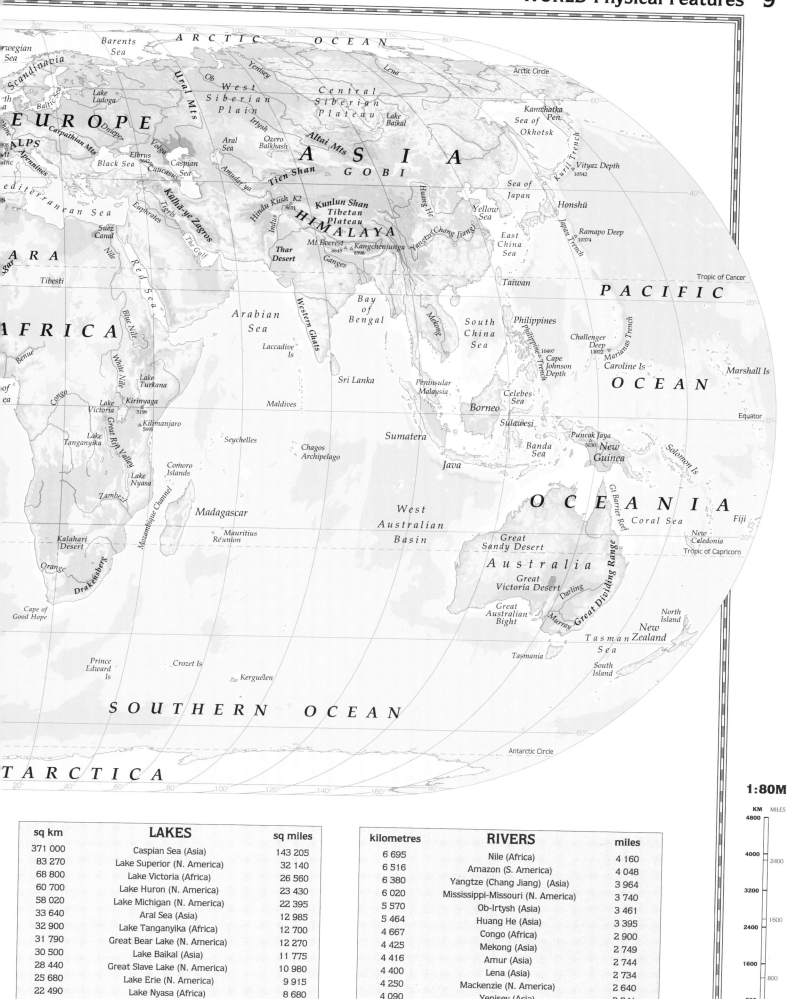

1:80M

sq km	LAKES	sq miles
371 000	Caspian Sea (Asia)	143 205
83 270	Lake Superior (N. America)	32 140
68 800	Lake Victoria (Africa)	26 560
60 700	Lake Huron (N. America)	23 430
58 020	Lake Michigan (N. America)	22 395
33 640	Aral Sea (Asia)	12 985
32 900	Lake Tanganyika (Africa)	12 700
31 790	Great Bear Lake (N. America)	12 270
30 500	Lake Baikal (Asia)	11 775
28 440	Great Slave Lake (N. America)	10 980
25 680	Lake Erie (N. America)	9 915
22 490	Lake Nyasa (Africa)	8 680

kilometres	RIVERS	miles
6 695	Nile (Africa)	4 160
6 516	Amazon (S. America)	4 048
6 380	Yangtze (Chang Jiang) (Asia)	3 964
6 020	Mississippi-Missouri (N. America)	3 740
5 570	Ob-Irtysh (Asia)	3 461
5 464	Huang He (Asia)	3 395
4 667	Congo (Africa)	2 900
4 425	Mekong (Asia)	2 749
4 416	Amur (Asia)	2 744
4 400	Lena (Asia)	2 734
4 250	Mackenzie (N. America)	2 640
4 090	Yenisey (Asia)	2 541

KM MILES
4800
4000 — 2400
3200
2400 — 1600
1600
800 — 800
0

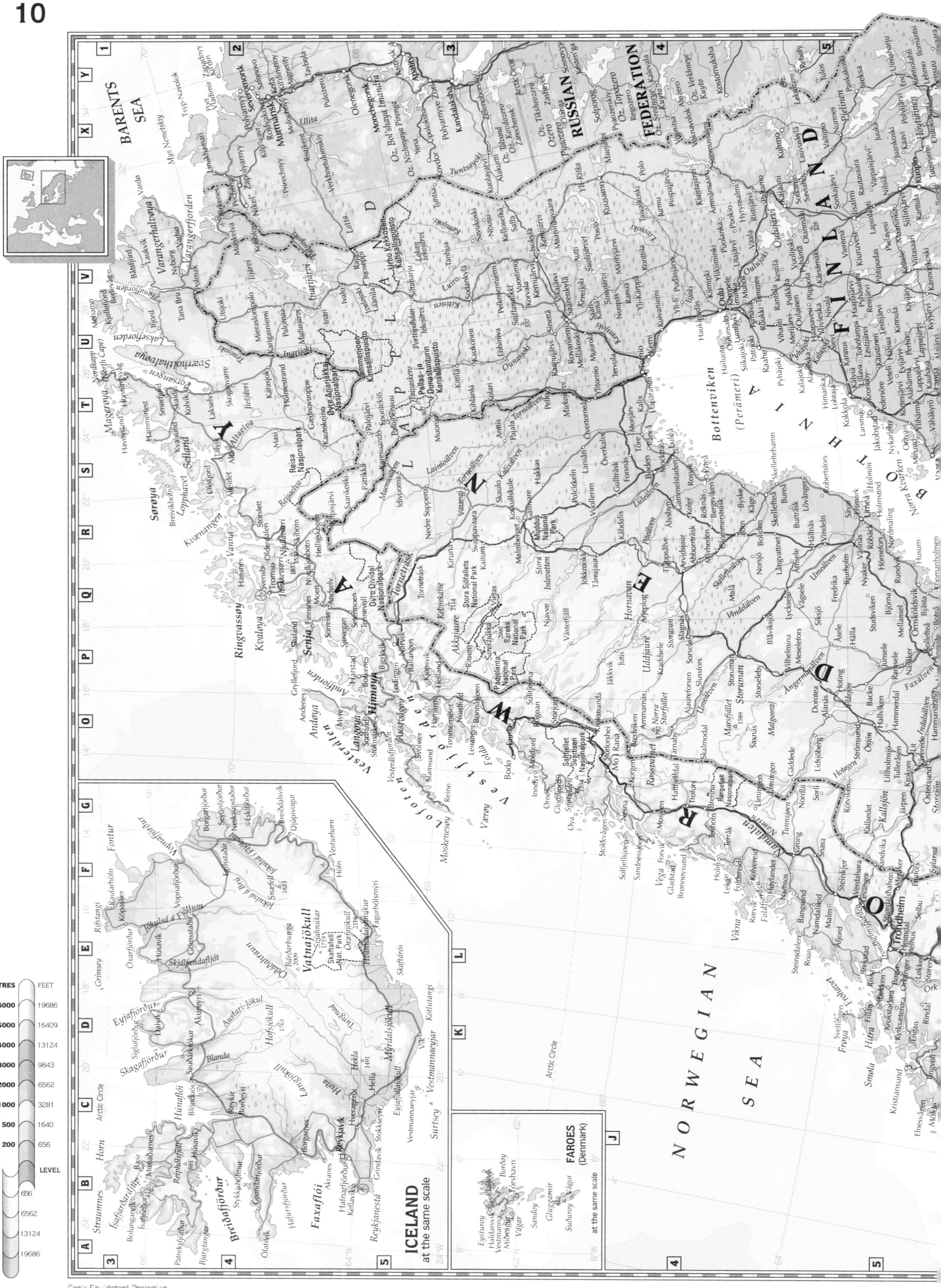

BARENTS SEA

RUSSIAN FEDERATION

FINLAND

LAPLAND

NORWAY

SWEDEN

NORWEGIAN SEA

METRES **FEET**
6000	19686
5000	16409
4000	13124
3000	9843
2000	6562
1000	3281
500	1640
200	656
SEA	LEVEL
200	656
2000	6562
4000	13124
6000	19686

ICELAND at the same scale

Vatnajökull
Skaftafell Nat. Park

FAROES (Denmark) at the same scale

Tórshavn

Arctic Circle

1:5M

© Collins

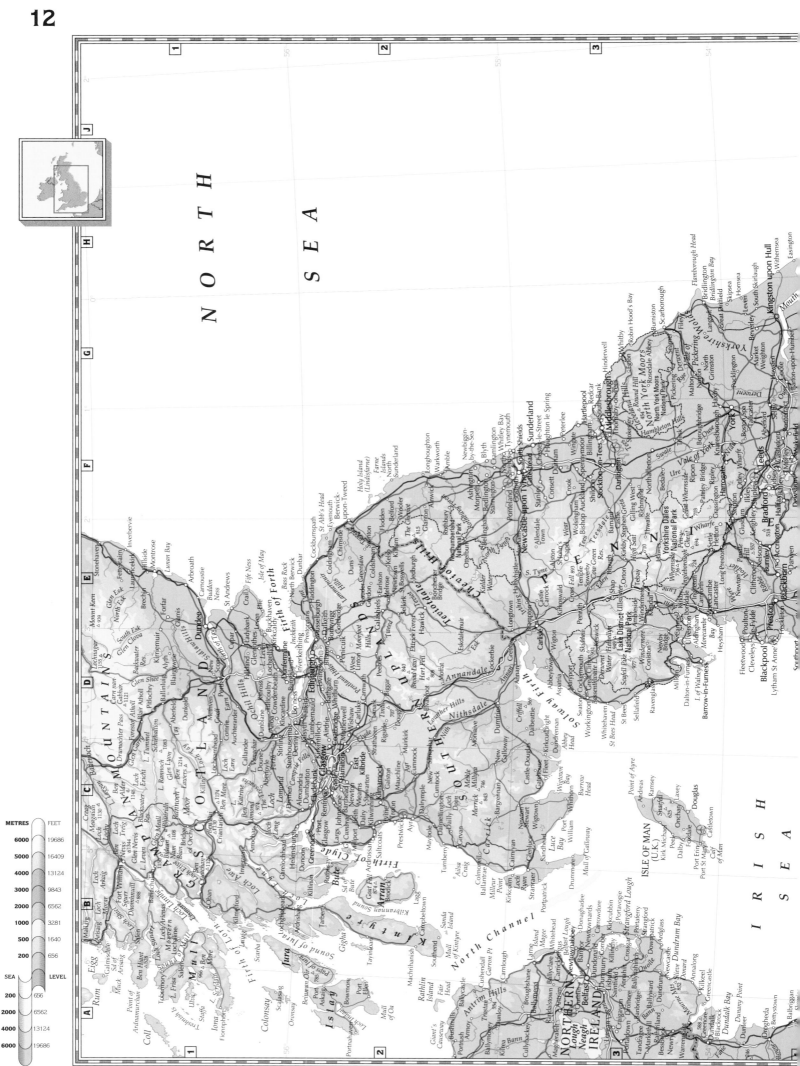

Conic Equidistant Projection

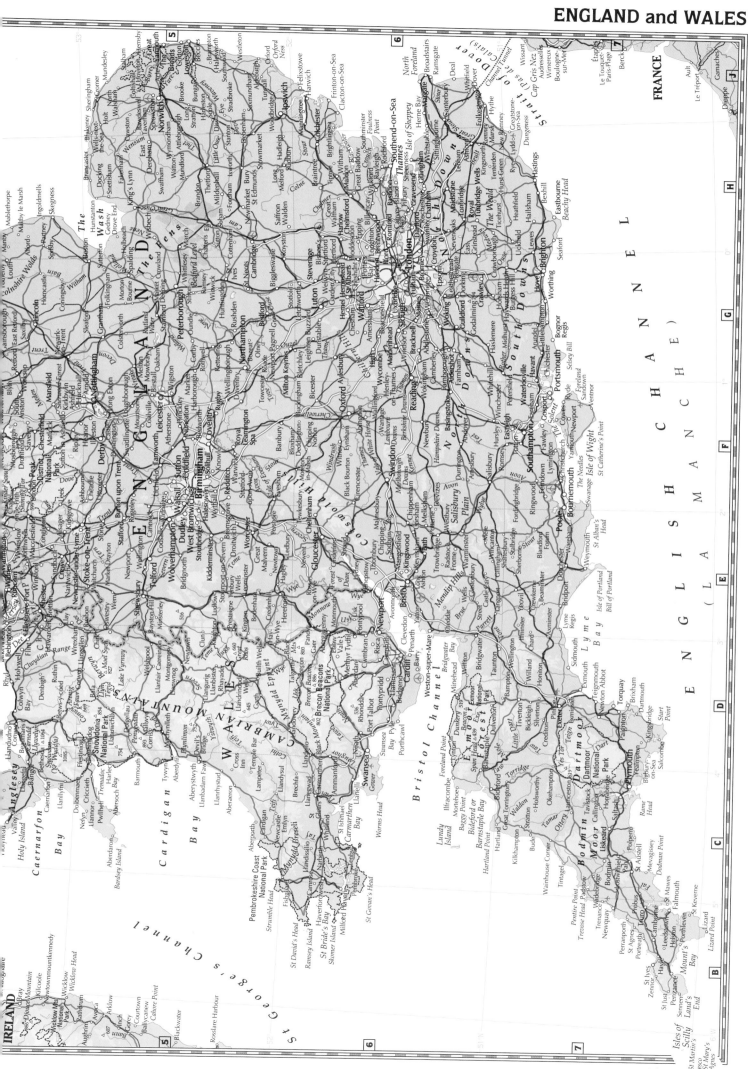

1:2M

KM MILES

ATLANTIC OCEAN

1:2M

ATLANTIC
OCEAN

SCOTLAND

NORTHERN
IRELAND

Belfast

REPUBLIC
OF
IRELAND

Dublin

IRISH
SEA

Galway Bay

Limerick

Cork

St George's Channel

1:2M

Conic Equidistant Projection

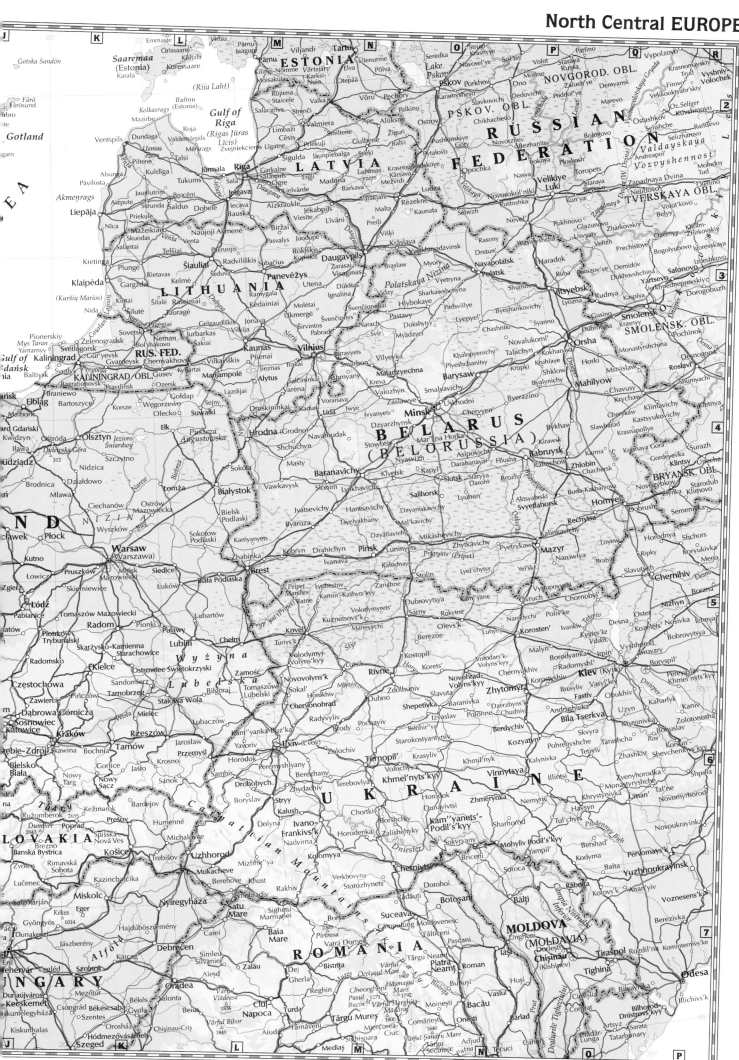

1:5M

KM	MILES
	200
300	
	150
250	
200	100
150	
	50
100	
50	
0	0

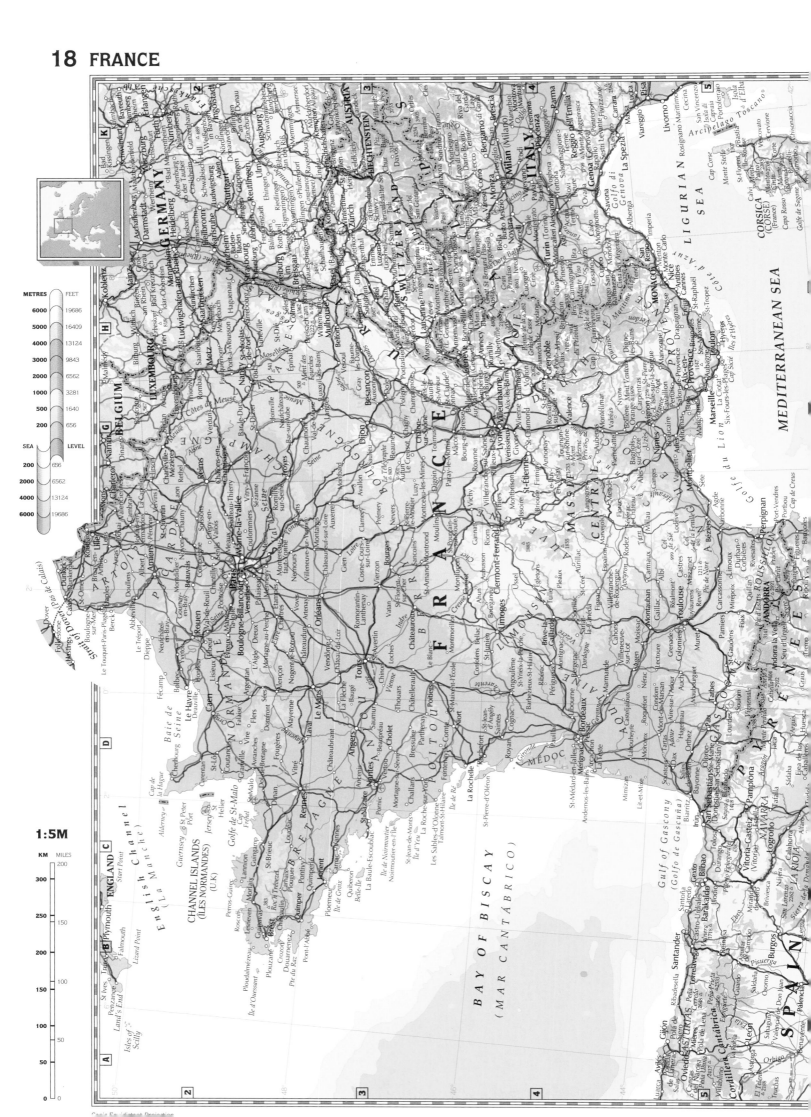

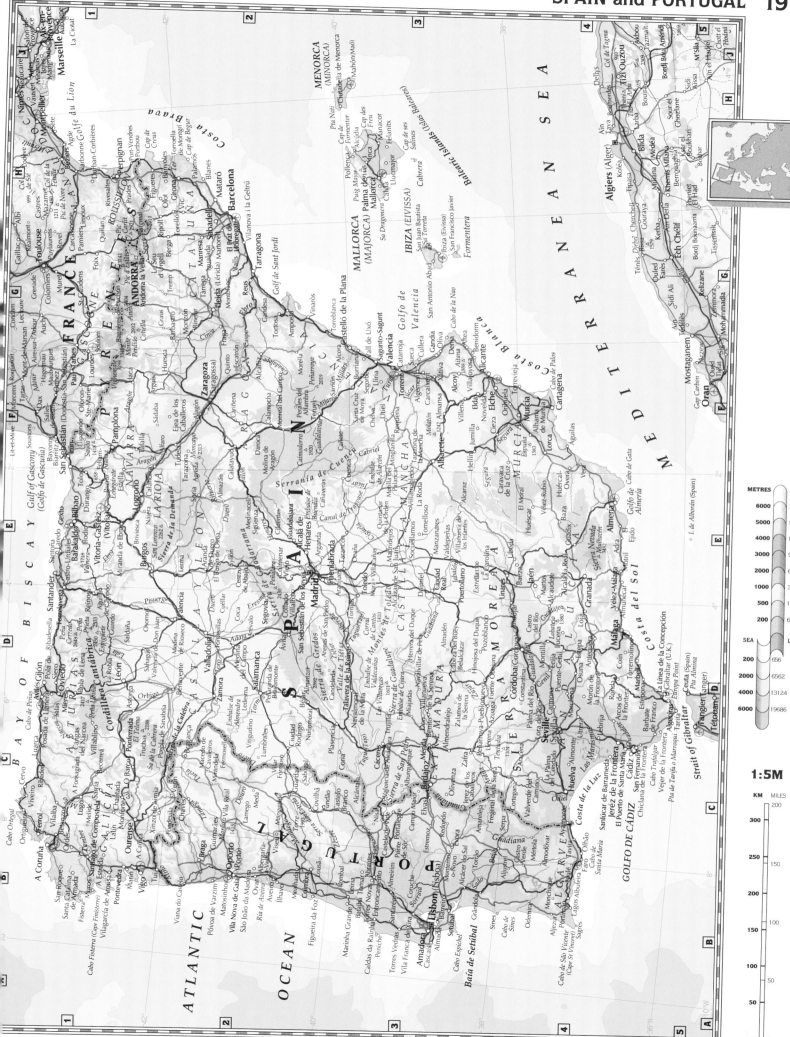

© Collins

1:5M

KM MILES
250
200
150
100
50
0

© Collins

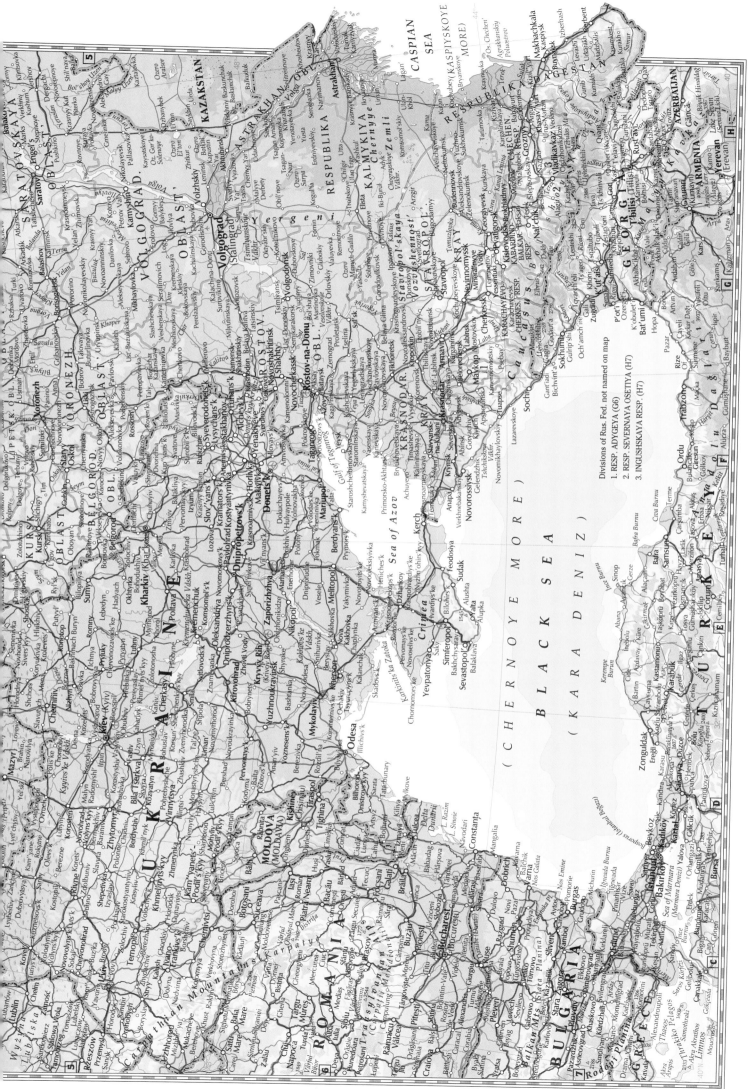

CASPIAN SEA (KASPIYSKOYE MORE)

KAZAKSTAN

SARATOVSKAYA OBLAST'

Saratov
Engel's

ASTRAKHAN' OBL.

Astrakhan'

VOLGOGRAD OBLAST'

Volgograd
Stalingrad

RESPUBLIKA KALMYKIYA Chernyye Zemli

Yergeni

Elista

DAGESTAN RESPUBLIKA

Makhachkala
Kaspiysk
Derbent

AZERBAIJAN

ARMENIA

Yerevan (Erevan)

GEORGIA

T'bilisi (Tbilisi)

ROSTOV. OBL.

Rostov-na-Donu
Shakhty
Novoshakhtinsk

Novocherkassk
Bataysk

STAVROPOL' KRAY

Stavropol'
Nevinnomyssk

Kislovodsk
Pyatigorsk
Yessentuki

KRASNODAR KRAY

Krasnodar
Armavir
Maykop

Novorossiysk

C a u c a s u s

CHECHEN RESP.
GROZNYY
Nal'chik
KABARDINO-
BALKAR. RESP.
Vladikavkaz

VORONEZH OBLAST'

Voronezh

LIPETSK OBL.

KURSK OBLAST'

Kursk

BELGOROD OBL.

Belgorod

U K R A I N E

Kharkiv (Khar'kov)
Luhans'k
Donets'k
Makiyivka
Horlivka
Mariupol'
Dnipropetrovs'k
Zaporizhzhya
Kryvyy Rih
Kremenchuk
Poltava
Sumy
Cherkasy
Kiev (Kyiv)
Zhytomyr
Vinnytsya
Khmel'nyts'kyy
Ternopil'
L'viv
Rivne
Luts'k
Kherson
Mykolayiv
Odesa
Sevastopol'
Simferopol'

Crimea

Sea of Azov

Taganrog
Kerch
Feodosiya
Sudak
Yalta

Gulf of Taganrog

MOLDOVA (MOLDAVA)

Kishinev
Chişinău
Tiraspol'

R O M A N I A

Bucharest

Iaşi
Galaţi
Brăila
Constanţa
Ploieşti
Craiova
Braşov
Cluj-Napoca
Timişoara
Sibiu
Arad
Oradea

Carpathian Mountains

Transylvanian Alps (Carpaţii Meridionali)

B U L G A R I A

Sofia
Plovdiv
Varna
Burgas
Ruse
Pleven
Stara Planina (Balkan Mts)

G R E E C E

T U R K E Y

Istanbul
Bursa
Samsun
Trabzon
Ordu
Zonguldak

Sea of Marmara (Marmara Denizi)

CHERNOYE MORE

BLACK SEA

(KARA DENIZ)

Divisions of Rus. Fed. not named on map
1. RESP. ADYGEYA (G6)
2. RESP. SEVERNAYA OSETIYA (H7)
3. INGUSHSKAYA RESP. (H7)

KARA- CHAYEVO- CHERKES. RESP.

1:7M

KM MILES
350
300   200
250
         150
200
150   100
100
50   50
0   0

© Collins

24

1:21M

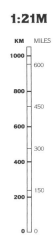

© Collins

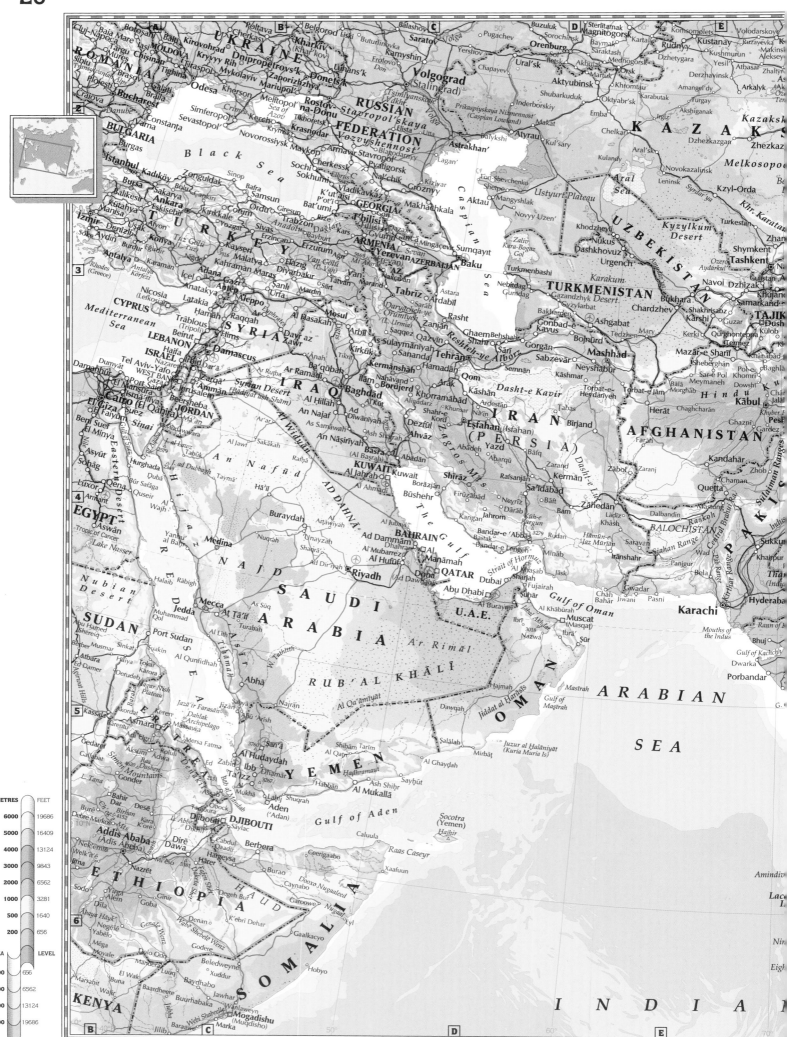

Albers Equal Area Conic Projection

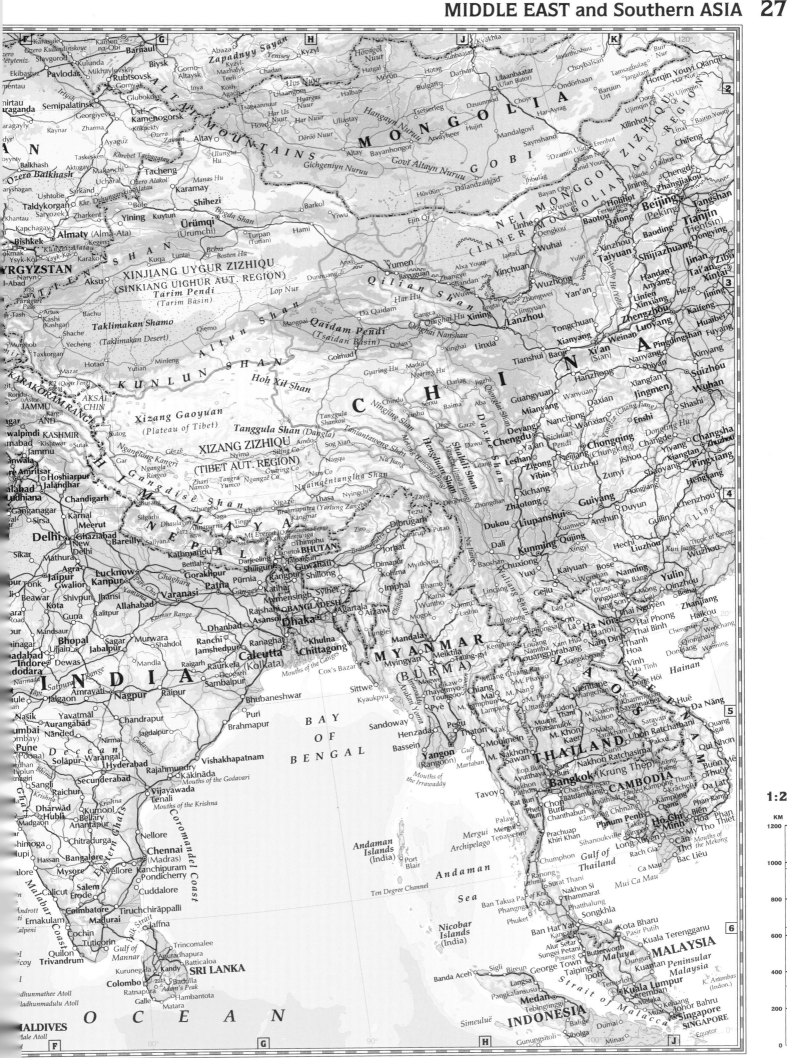

1:20M

KM   MILES
1200
              600
1000
800   400

600
              200
400

200

0

© Collins

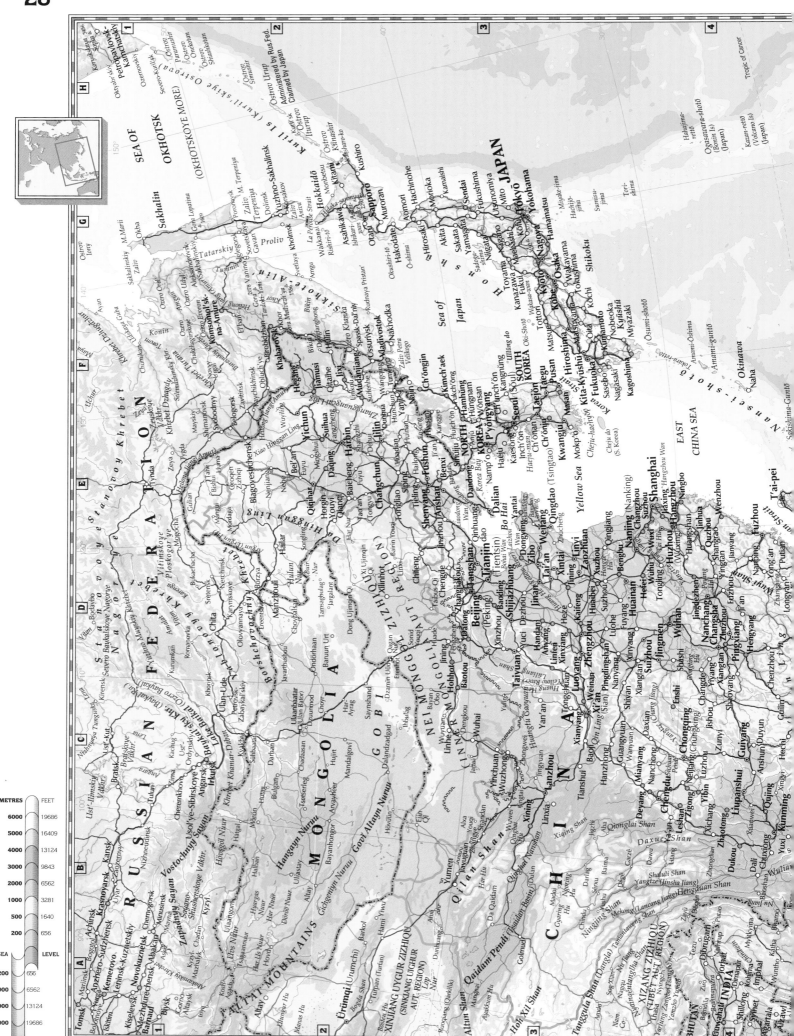

28

SEA OF OKHOTSK
(OKHOTSKOYE MORE)

Kuril'Is (Kuril'skiye Ostrova)
Administered by Rus.Fed.
Claimed by Japan

JAPAN

Sakhalin

RUSSIAN FEDERATION

MONGOLIA

Ulaanbaatar (Ulan Bator)

GOBI

Ürümqi (Urumchi)

XINJIANG UYGUR ZIZHIQU
(SINKIANG UIGHUR AUT. REGION)

ALTAI MOUNTAINS

NEI MONGGOL ZIZHIQU
(INNER MONGOLIA AUT. REGION)

CHINA

Beijing (Peking)
Tianjin (Tientsin)

Qilian Shan

Qaidam Pendi (Tsaidam Basin)

XIZANG ZIZHIQU
(TIBET AUT. REGION)

Tanggula Shan (Dangla)

BHUTAN

INDIA

NEPAL

NORTH KOREA
P'yongyang

SOUTH KOREA
Seoul (Soul)

Yellow Sea

EAST CHINA SEA

Shanghai

Nanjing (Nanking)

Chongqing (Chungking)

Hokkaidō
Sapporo

Tōkyō
Yokohama

Sea of Japan

Kyūshū

Okinawa

Nansei-shotō

Tai-pei

Tropic of Cancer

METRES	FEET
6000	19686
5000	16409
4000	13124
3000	9843
2000	6562
1000	3281
500	1640
200	656
SEA	LEVEL
200	656
2000	6562
4000	13124
6000	19686

Conic Equidistant Projection

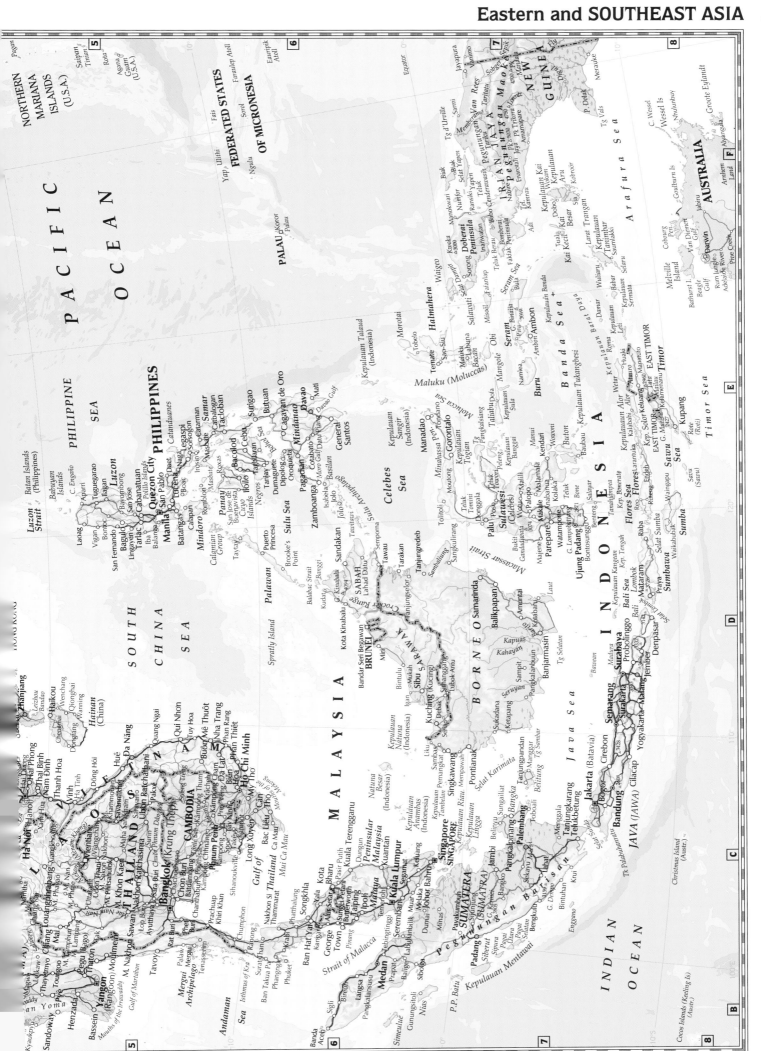

PACIFIC OCEAN

NORTHERN MARIANA ISLANDS (U.S.A.)

FEDERATED STATES OF MICRONESIA

PALAU

PHILIPPINE SEA

PHILIPPINES

Luzon Strait

Luzon

Manila
Quezon City
San Pablo

Mindoro

Samar

Leyte

Cebu

Panay

Negros

Palawan

SOUTH CHINA SEA

SABAH

SARAWAK

BRUNEI
Bandar Seri Begawan

MALAYSIA

BORNEO

Kota Kinabalu

Celebes Sea

Sulu Sea

Zamboanga

Davao

Mindanao

General Santos

Manado

Sulawesi (Celebes)

Halmahera

Maluku (Moluccas)

Molucca Sea

Ceram Sea

Seram

Buru

Ambon

Banda Sea

IRIAN JAYA

NEW GUINEA

Jayapura

Equator

Arafura Sea

AUSTRALIA

Darwin

Timor Sea

EAST TIMOR

Timor

INDONESIA

Flores Sea

Flores

Sumba

Sumbawa

Bali

Lombok

Java Sea

Makassar Strait

Balikpapan

Samarinda

Banjarmasin

Pontianak

Kuching

Ujung Padang

Surabaya
Semarang
Surakarta
Yogyakarta
Malang

Jakarta (Batavia)
Bandung
Cirebon

JAVA (JAWA)

SUMATERA (SUMATRA)

Palembang

Medan

Padang

Pekanbaru

INDIAN OCEAN

Singapore
SINGAPORE

Kuala Lumpur

Peninsular Malaysia

Strait of Malacca

George Town

THAILAND

Bangkok (Krung Thep)

Gulf of Thailand

CAMBODIA

Phnom Penh

Ho Chi Minh

VIETNAM

LAOS

Vientiane

Hanoi

Hai Phong

Da Nang

Yangon (Rangoon)

Hainan (China)

Zhanjiang

Haikou

Andaman Sea

1:20M

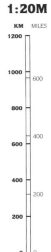

KM   MILES
1200
1000   600
800
600   400
400
200   200
0   0

© Collins

Conic Equidistant Projection

1:4M

NAURU
Yaren

Banaba
(Kiribati)
Aránuka
Howland
Island
(U.S.A.)
Baker Island
(U.S.A.)

Lyra Reef
ga Is
Nuguria Is
Feni Is
Kilinailau Is
Tauu
(Mortlock Is)
Nukumanu
Is
George
uka I.
ohano
Arawa
Bougainville
Island
Choiseul
Treasury
Is
Vella Lavella
Kolombangara
New Georgia Is
(Solomon Is)
lark I.
Rendova
Russell Is
New
Georgia
The Slot
Santa Isabel
Buala
Malu'u
Malaita
Maramasike
Ullawa I.
Ulawa I.

Ontong
Java Atoll
Roncador
Reef

SOLOMON
ISLANDS

Nonouti
Gilbert
Islands
(Kiribati)
Tabiteuea
Beru
Nikunau
Onotoa
Kingsmill Group
Tamana
Arorae

KIRIBATI

Phoenix Islands
McKean
Island
Kanton
Island

Nikumaroro

Orona
(Kiribati)
Manra

Equator
0°

1

Honiara
Guadalcanal
Avuavu
Kirakira
San Cristobal
Santa Ana
Rennell
Indispensable
Reefs

Duff Is
Swallow Is
Nupani
Ndeni
Santa Cruz Islands
(Solomon Is)
Utupua
Vanikoro Is
Cherry Island
Tikopia Mitre Island

Nanumea
Nanumanga
Niutao

Nui

Nukufetau
Vaitupu
TUVALU
Nukulaelae
Fongafale
Funafuti

Nukulaelae

Niulakita

Atafu
Nukunono
TOKELAU
(N.Z.)
Fakaofo

2

CORAL SEA

Torres
Islands
Uréparapara
Banks
Vanua Lava
Santa María I.
Islands

Espíritu Santo
Tabwémasana
1874
Aoba
Maéwo

Rotuma
(Fiji)

Íles
Wallis

WALLIS
AND FUTUNA IS
(Fr.)
Íles de Horn

SAMOA
Savaii
Apia
Upolu

3°

VANUATU
Malo
Pentecost I.
Norsup
Ambrym
Malakula
Epi
Émaé
Shepherd Is
Efaté
Vila

Íles Chesterfield
(New Caledonia)
Récifs
d'Entrecasteaux
Grand Passage
Íles Bélep
Grand
Récif
des
Français
Récif
de Cook
Koumac
Ouvéa
Erromango
Tanna
Aniwa
Futuna
Anatom
(Vanuatu)

NEW CALEDONIA
(NOUVELLE CALÉDONIE)
(Fr.)
Lifou
Tadine
Yaté
Íles Loyauté
(Loyalty Is)
(Fr.)
Maré

Nouméa
Grand Récif
du Sud

Í. de Sable

Yasawa
Group
Great Sea Reef
Labasa
Vanua
Levu
Lautoka
Bligh
Water
Koro
Viti Levu
Nadi
Ovalau
Korò
Sea
Suva
1324
Koro
Gau
FIJI
Beqa
Moala
Kadavu Passage
Lakeba
Kadavu
Matuku

Niuatoputopu
(Tonga)
Tafahi
(Tonga)

Tutuila
(U.S.A.)

Hunter I.
(Fr.)
Conway
Reef
(Fiji)
Ono-i-Lau
(Fiji)

Tofua
Vava'u
Group
TONGA

Niue
(N.Z.)

20°

y Cape
Bay
Island
orough

Ata
(Tonga)

Nuku'alofa
Tongatapu
Group

Horizon
Depth
10882

Tropic of Capricorn

ntin
ture
bane
leigh
ld Coast
ron Bay
llina

Harbour
ille
acquarie

Norfolk
Island
(Aust.)

SOUTH

4

Lord Howe
Island
(Aust.)

PACIFIC

TASMAN SEA

OCEAN

Three Kings Is
Cape Maria van Diemen
North Cape
Whangarei

30°

Kaipara Harbour
Takapuna
Manukau
Auckland
Bay of
Plenty
Great Barrier
Island

NORTH
ISLAND

Hamilton
Tauranga
Tokoroa
East Cape
1754
Hikurangi
North Taranaki Bight
New Plymouth
Mt Egmont (Mt Taranaki)
2518
Lake
Taupo
Gisborne
Wairoa
Mahia Peninsula
South Taranaki Bight
Napier
Cape Farewell
Wanganui
Hastings
Hawke Bay

1:20M

Karamea Bight
Nelson
Westport
Blenheim
Greymouth
Hokitika
Palmerston North
Masterton
Lower Hutt
Wellington
Cape
Palliser

Cook Strait

NEW ZEALAND

5

KM MILES
1200
800

Mt Cook (Mt Aoraki)
3754
Southern Alps
Pegasus Bay
Christchurch
Banks Peninsula
Mt Aspiring
Mt Christina
2030
Lake Pukaki
Lake Tekapo
Canterbury Bight
1000
600
800

Resolution Island
Cape Providence
Lake Te Anau
Lake
Wanaka
Lake
Wakatipu
Oamaru
Otago Peninsula
Dunedin
SOUTH ISLAND
Chatham
Islands
(N.Z.)
600
400

Stewart Island
Invercargill
Foveaux Strait
South West Cape
Pitt I.

400
200

Snares Is
Bounty
Islands

6

200

Auckland Is

0

© Collins

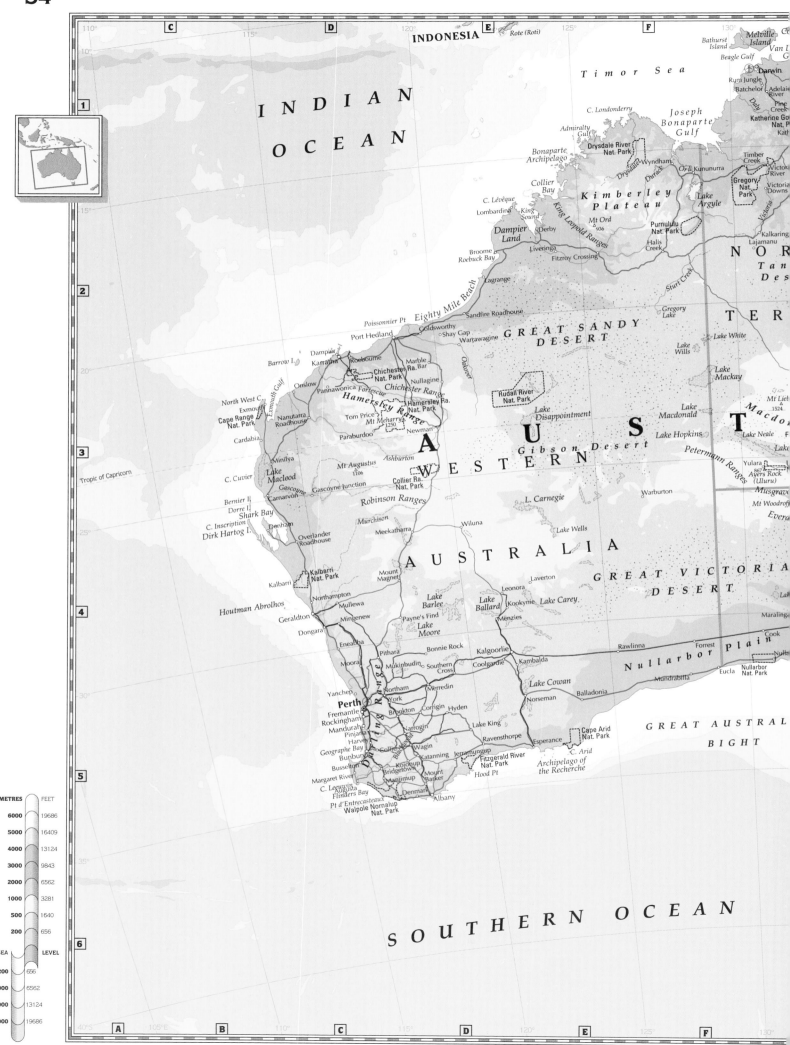

INDONESIA
Rote (Roti)

INDIAN

OCEAN

Timor Sea

Bathurst
Island
Melville
Island
Van I
G
Beagle Gulf
Darwin
Rum Jungle
Batchelor
Pine
Katherine Go
Nat. P
Kath

C. Londonderry
Joseph
Bonaparte
Gulf

Admiralty
Gulf

Bonaparte
Archipelago
Drysdale River
Nat. Park
Drysdale
Wyndham
Durack
Ord
Kununurra
Victoria
River

Gregory
Nat.
Park
Victoria
Downs

Collier
Bay
C. Lévêque
Lombardina
King
Sound
Kimberley
Plateau
King Leopold Ranges
Mt Ord
936
Lake
Argyle

Kalkarin

Dampier
Land
Derby
Purnululu
Nat. Park

NOR

Broome
Liveringa
Halls
Creek

Tan
Des

Roebuck Bay
Fitzroy Crossing

Lagrange
Sturt Creek
TER

Poissonnier Pt
Eighty Mile Beach
Sandfire Roadhouse

Gregory
Lake

Port Hedland
Goldsworthy
GREAT SANDY
Lake White

Dampier
Karratha
Roebourne
Shay Gap
Wartawagine
DESERT
Lake
Wills
Lake
Mackay

Barrow I.
Marble
Bar
Nullagine
Oakover

Chichester Ra.
Nat. Park

Chichester Range
North West C.
Onslow
Pannawonica
Fortescue
Hamersley Range
Hamersley Ra.
Nat. Park
Rudall River
Nat. Park
Lake
Macdonald
Mt Lieb
1524
Macdo

Exmouth
Cape Range
Nat. Park
Nanutarra
Roadhouse
Tom Price
Mt Meharry
1250
Newman
Lake
Disappointment
Lake
Hopkins
Lake Neale

Cardabia
Paraburdoo
A U S T

Minilya
Ashburton
Gibson Desert
Petermann Ranges
Yulara
867
Ayers Rock
(Uluru)

Mt Augustus
1106
W E S T E R N
Warburton
Musgrave
Mt Woodrof
Evera

C. Cuvier
Lake
Macleod
Gascoyne Junction
Collier Ra.
Nat. Park

Bernier I.
Gascoyne
Robinson Ranges
L. Carnegie

Dorre I.
Carnarvon
Murchison
C. Inscription
Shark Bay
Denham
Meekatharra
Wiluna
Lake Wells

Dirk Hartog I.
Overlander
Roadhouse

A U S T R A L I A

Kalbarri
Nat. Park
Mount
Magnet
Laverton
GREAT VICTORIA

Kalbarri
Northampton
Lake
Barlee
Lake
Ballard
Leonora
Kookynie
Lake Carey
DESERT

Houtman Abrolhos
Mullewa
Payne's Find
Menzies
Cook

Geraldton
Mingenew
Lake
Moore
Maraling

Dongara
Eneabba
Pithara
Bonnie Rock
Kalgoorlie
Rawlinna
Forrest
Nullarbor Plain
Nulla

Moora
Mukinbudin
Southern
Cross
Coolgardie
Kambalda
Nullarbor
Nat. Park

Yanchep
Northam
Merredin
Lake Cowan
Mundrabilla
Eucla

Perth
York
Brookton
Corrigin
Hyden
Norseman
Balladonia

Fremantle
Rockingham
Mandurah
Pinjarra
Harvey
Narrogin
Lake King
GREAT AUSTRAL

Geographe Bay
Bunbury
Collie
Wagin
Ravensthorpe
Esperance
Cape Arid
Nat. Park
BIGHT

Busselton
Bridgetown
Koloup
Katanning
Jerramungup
Fitzgerald River
Nat. Park
C. Arid
Archipelago of
the Recherche

Margaret River
Manjimup
Mount
Barker
Hood Pt

C. Leeuwin
Augusta
Flinders Bay
Denmark
Albany
Pt d'Entrecasteaux
Walpole Nornalup
Nat. Park

Darling Range

Tropic of Capricorn

SOUTHERN OCEAN

Lambert Azimuthal Equal Area Projection

METRES	FEET
6000	19686
5000	16409
4000	13124
3000	9843
2000	6562
1000	3281
500	1640
200	656
SEA	LEVEL
200	656
2000	6562
4000	13124
6000	19686

PAPUA
NEW GUINEA

CORAL SEA

Gulf of
Carpentaria

Cape
York
Peninsula

QUEENSLAND

GREAT DIVIDING RANGE

Simpson
Desert

NEW SOUTH
WALES

VICTORIA

Adelaide

Melbourne

Brisbane

Gold Coast

Sydney
Wollongong

Canberra
A.C.T.

TASMAN

SEA

Bass Strait

TASMANIA

Hobart

1:13M

© Collins

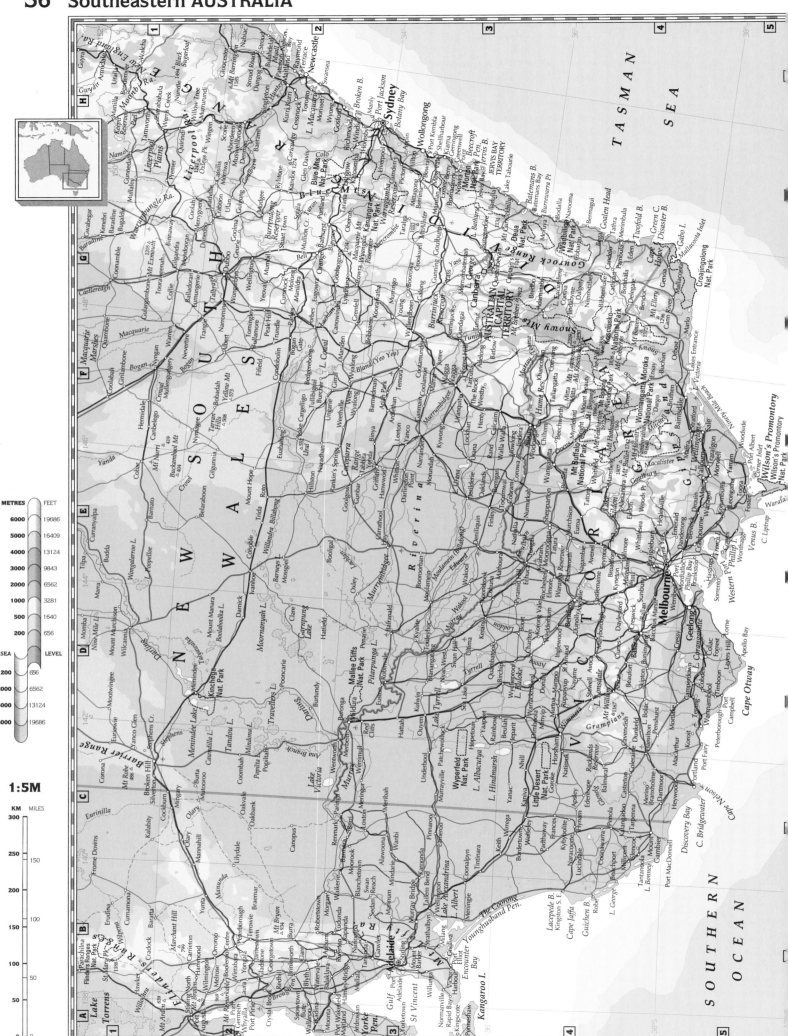

1:5M

Lambert Azimuthal Equal Area Projection

Three Kings Is

Cape Reinga   North Cape
Cape Maria van Diemen   Te Paki
Te Kao
Parengarenga Harbour
C. Karikari
Rangaunu Bay   Doubtless Bay
Awanui   Kaeo   Bay of Islands   Cape Brett
Ahipara Bay   Kaitaia   Kerikeri   Russell
Tauroa Pt   Ahipara   Kawakawa   Towai
Broadwood
Poor Knights Is
Hokianga Harbour   Taheke
Pakotai   Whangarei
Donnellys Crossing
Bream Bay   Mokohinau Is
Dargaville   Little Barrier   Port Fitzroy
Tangaehe   Maungaturoto   Great Barrier Island
Wellsford Leigh   Colville Chan.   Mercury Islands
North Head   Warkworth   Colville   Coromandel   Whitianga
Kaipara Harbour   Otewa   Kawau I.   Peninsula   The Aldermen Is
East Coast Bays   Waiheke I.
Takapuna   Oneroa   Whangamata
Auckland   Papatoetoe   Thames
Manukau   Kohukohunui 688   837   Mayor I.   Bay of   Cape Runaway
Manukau Harbour   Papakura   Waitakaruru   Whakatane   Hicks Bay
Pukekohe   Paeroa   Waihi   Matakana I.   White I.   Te Araroa
Waiuku   L. Aroha   Katikati   Motiti I.   Waikawa Pt   East Cape
Port Waikato   Huntly   Waitoa   Tauranga   Plenty   Hikurangi 1754
Glen Afton   Te Puke   Rotorua Teko   Ruatoria
Ngaruawahia   Waiharoa   Whakatane   Tokomaru Bay
Hamilton   Cambridge   Kawerau   Taneatua   Mawhai Pt
Kawhia   Te Awamutu   Rotorua   Opotiki   Tolaga Bay
Kawhia Harbour   Otorohanga   Kaingaroa   1213
Te Kuiti   Tokoroa   Mt Tarawera   Murupara   Matawai   679
Awakino   Mokau   Mangakino   Mt Edgecumbe   Urewera   Gisborne
North   Aria   Pacoa   Taupo   Nat. Park   Poverty Bay
Taranaki Bight   1111   Waitahanui   Rangitaiki   523   Table
Waitara   Okahukura   Hauhungaroa   Turangi   1369   Kaitawa   Cape
New Plymouth   Ohura   1078   Lake Taupo   Mohaka   Frasertown
Whangamomona   Mt Ngauruhoe   Tarawera   Bay View
Cape Egmont   2291   Mt Ruapehu   Waipuru   Nuhaka   Napier
Mt Egmont   Egmont   Tongariro Nat. Park   746   2797   Kaimanawa   Mahia Pen.
(Mt Taranaki) 2518   Nat. Park   Mt Ruapehu   Mts   Portland I.
Opunake   Stratford   Ohakune   Waiouru   Hawke   Bay
Hawera   Raetihi   Wairoa
South   Patea   Taihape   Hastings   C. Kidnappers
Taranaki Bight   Wanganui   Mangaweka   Tikokino
Turakina   Ongaonga   Waimarama
Marton   Waipawa
Feilding   Kimbolton   Takapau   Waipukurau
Rongotea   Woodville   803   Dannevirke
Palmerston North   Porangahau
Foxton
Cape Farewell   Farewell Spit   Levin   Eketahuna   Cape Turnagain
Collingwood   Cape Stephens   Otaki   1571
Golden Bay   Kapiti I.   Pongaroa
Kahurangi Pt   Takaka   Separation Pt   Paraparaumu   Mitre   Castlepoint
Aorere   D'Urville I.   Porirua   Masterton
Abel Tasman   Upper Takaka   French   Upper   Leatherston   Te Wharau
Nat. Park   Pass   Hutt   Flat Point
Tasman   Riwaka   Tasman   Picton   Wellington   Mt Ross   Flat Point
Karamea   Mts   Bay   Canvastown   Lower   Wairarapa   564
Karamea Bight   Richmond   Nelson   Cloudy B.   Hutt   Palliser   983
Wakefield   1760   Blenheim   Bay   Cape Palliser
Cape Foulwind   Hope   Richmond   Renwick   Seddon
Saddle   Mt Tuamarina   Clifford B.
Waimangaroa   Owen River   Wairau   Cape Campbell
Westport   Buller   Pinnacle   Cook
Inangahua   2131   St Arnaud Range   Strait
Charleston   Junction   Mt   1832   Travers   Inland Kaikoura Range
Reefton   2338   Clarence   Tapuaenuku
Runanga   Mt Ajax   Hope   2885   Clarence   2610
Greymouth   1832   Springs   Waiau   Manakau
Springs   Kaikoura   Parnassus
Ahaura   Junction   Hanmer   Kaikoura Peninsula
Hokitika   L. Brunner   Springs   Oaro
L. Kaniere   L. Sumner   Rotherham   Cheviot
Kowhitirangi   Otira   Mt Crossley   Culverden   Waipara
Ross   Arthur's   1987   Hurunui   Waikari
Abut Head   2195   Arthur's Pass   Hawarden
Harihari   Nat. Park   L. Coleridge   Rangiora   Pegasus
Franz Josef   Mt Arrowsmith   Kaiapoi   Bay
Glacier   2795   Oxford   Belfast
Fox Glacier   Mt Elie de   Coalgate   Christchurch
Mt Cook   Beaumont   Sheffield   Sumner
(Mt Aoraki)   3750   Mt Cook   Aylesbury   Taitapu
Westland Nat. Park   Nat. Park   Te Pirita   Rolleston   Banks
Haast   Mt   2644   Mayfield   Southbridge   Peninsula
Lake   Cook   Lake Tekapo   Lake   Akaroa
Jackson Head   Paringa   Mt Ward   Akaroa Harb.
Cascade Pt   Pukaki   Burke   Canterbury   Ellesmere
Mt Aspiring   2499   Lake Pukaki   Plains   Ashburton
Awarua Pt   Nat. Park   Pass   Geraldine   Canterbury
Pleasant   Bight
Milford Sd   Mt Aspiring   3033   Point
Milford Sound   3027   Mt Alta   Temuka
George Sd   2347   Benmore   Timaru
Omarama   Pareora
Wanaka   SOUTH ISLAND
Caswell Sd   Fiordland   L. Wanaka   Kurow   Waimate
National Park   Pisa   2087   Studholme Junction
Secretary I.   1879   Mts   Kakanui   Glenavy   SOUTH PACIFIC
Doubtful Sd   Te Anau   Cardrona   1643   Mts   Pukeuri Junction
Breaksea   Queenstown   Cromwell   Naseby   C. Wanbrow   OCEAN
Sd   L. Manapouri   Arrowtown   Alexandra   Hyde   Oamaru
Resolution   Mt Ward   Roxburgh   Hampden
I.   L. Te Anau   Eyre Mts   Moeraki
Caroline Pt   Athol   Clutha   Middlemarch   Shag Pt
Cape   722   Lake Wakatipu   Lumsden   Palmerston
wilderness   Ohai   Kingston   Roxburgh   Waikouaiti
alky In.   Winton   Mossburn   Port Chalmers
Puysegur   Poteriteri   Mataura   Dipton   Waipahi   Dunedin
Pt   Te Waewae   Balfour   Beaumont   Mosgiel   Otago Peninsula
Bay   Orepuki   Mandeville   Brighton
Riverton   Otautau   Gore   Milton
Pahia Pt   Edendale   Waipahi   Balclutha
Invercargill   Mt Pye   Owaka   Kaitangata
Foveaux   Waikawa   Nugget Pt
Codfish I.   980   Bluff   Waipapa   Long Pt
Halfmoon   Toetoes   Papatowai
Mason B.   Bay   Ruapuke I.   Waipapa Pt   Chaslands Mistake
Shelter Pt
Stewart Island
Muttonbird Is   South West Cape

TASMAN
SEA

NORTH ISLAND

SOUTH ISLAND

SOUTH PACIFIC
OCEAN

Cook Strait

Southern Alps

Canterbury Plains

METRES	FEET
6000	19686
5000	16409
4000	13124
3000	9843
2000	6562
1000	3281
500	1640
200	656
SEA	LEVEL
200	656
2000	6562
4000	13124
6000	19686

1:5M

KM	MILES
300	200
250	150
200	100
150	50
100	
50	
0	0

Equidistant Projection

© Collins

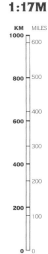

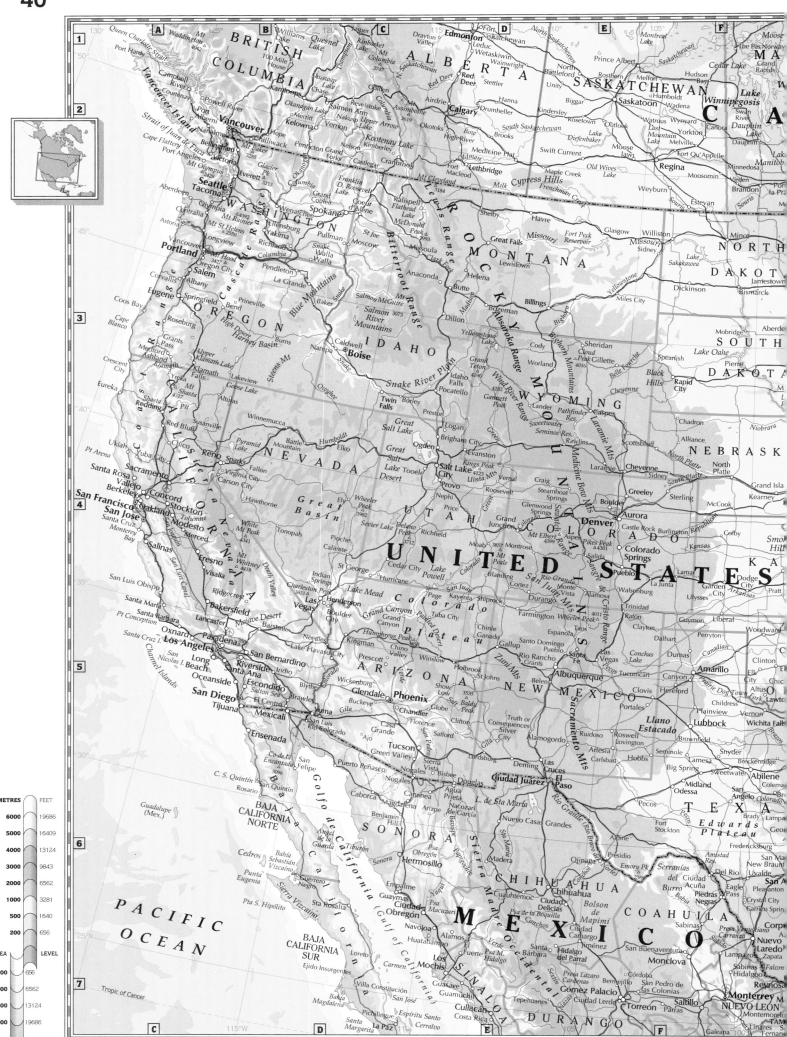

Lambert Conformal Conic Projection

METRES	FEET
6000	19686
5000	16409
4000	13124
3000	9843
2000	6562
1000	3281
500	1640
200	656
SEA	LEVEL
200	656
2000	6562
4000	13124
6000	19686

1:12M

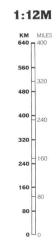

© Collins

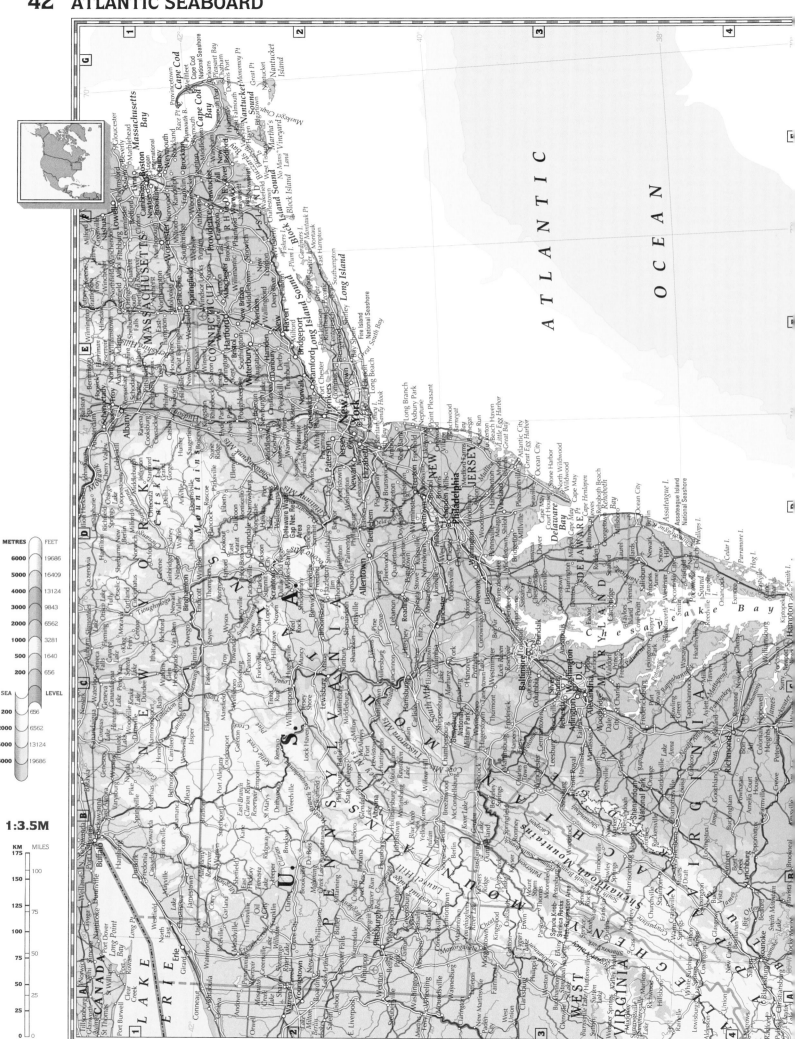

1:3.5M

Lambert Conformal Conic Projection

Lambert Conformal Conic Projection

1:3.5M

METRES		FEET
6000		19686
5000		16409
4000		13124
3000		9843
2000		6562
1000		3281
500		1640
200		656
SEA		LEVEL
200		656
2000		6562
4000		13124
6000		19686

KM	MILES
175	100
150	
125	75
100	
75	50
50	
25	25

ATLANTIC

OCEAN

CARIBBEAN SEA

BERMUDA
(U.K.) ●Hamilton

Tropic of Cancer

NORTH CAROLINA

SOUTH CAROLINA

GEORGIA

THE BAHAMAS

CUBA

HISPANIOLA

HAITI

DOMINICAN
REPUBLIC

PUERTO
RICO
(U.S.A.)

LEEWARD ISLANDS

VIRGIN IS
(U.K.)

VIRGIN IS
(U.S.A.)

ANGUILLA

ANTIGUA
AND
BARBUDA

ST KITTS-NEVIS

MONTSERRAT
(U.K.)

GUADELOUPE
(Fr.)

DOMINICA

MARTINIQUE
(Fr.)

ST LUCIA

ST VINCENT &
THE GRENADINES

BARBADOS

GRENADA

TRINIDAD
AND
TOBAGO

JAMAICA

CAYMAN
ISLANDS
(U.K.)

GREATER ANTILLES

Lesser Antilles

WINDWARD ISLANDS

NETHERLANDS
ANTILLES

ARUBA
(Neth.)

VENEZUELA

PANAMA

COSTA RICA

COLOMBIA

Cordillera Oriental

1:14M

KM 700
MILES
600   400
500   300
400
300   200
200
100   100
0   0

© Collins

PACIFIC OCEAN

COSTA RICA

NICARAGUA

PANAMA

COLOMBIA

VENEZUELA

ECUADOR

PERU

BOLIVIA

ARGENTINA

Lesser Antilles

NETHERLANDS ANTILLES

GALAPAGOS IS
(Ecuador)
at the same scale

METRES	FEET
6000	19686
5000	16409
4000	13124
3000	9843
2000	6562
1000	3281
500	1640
200	656
SEA	LEVEL
200	656
2000	6562
4000	13124
6000	19686

Lambert Azimuthal Equal Area Projection

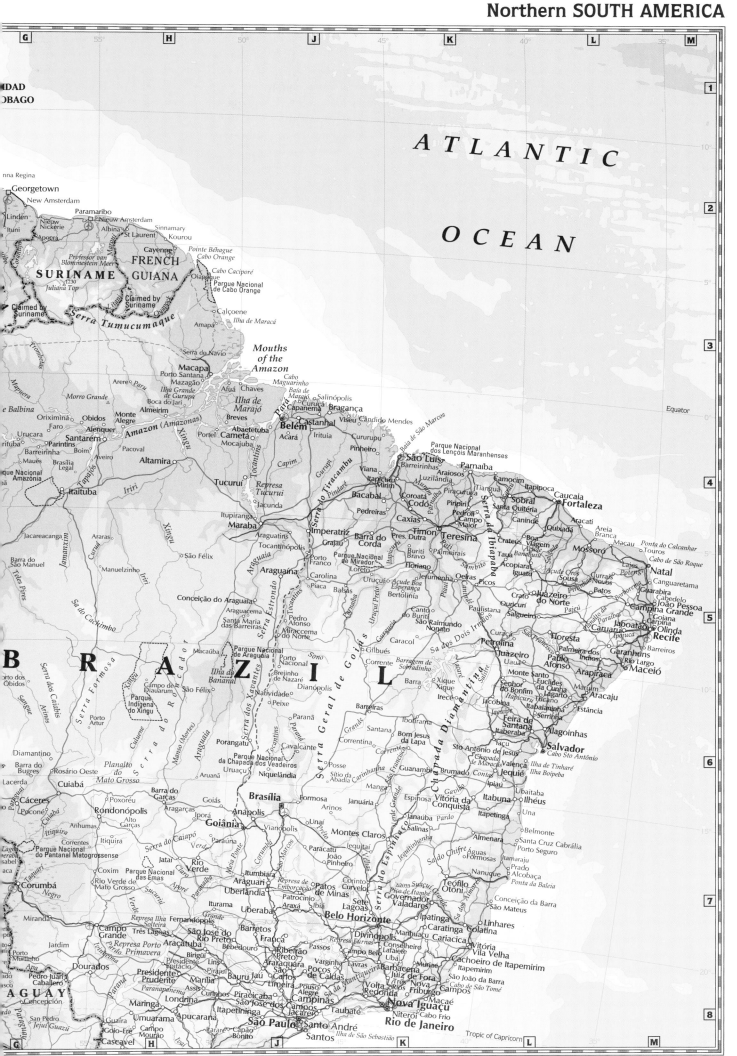

ATLANTIC

OCEAN

1:15M

Tropic of Capricorn

© Collins

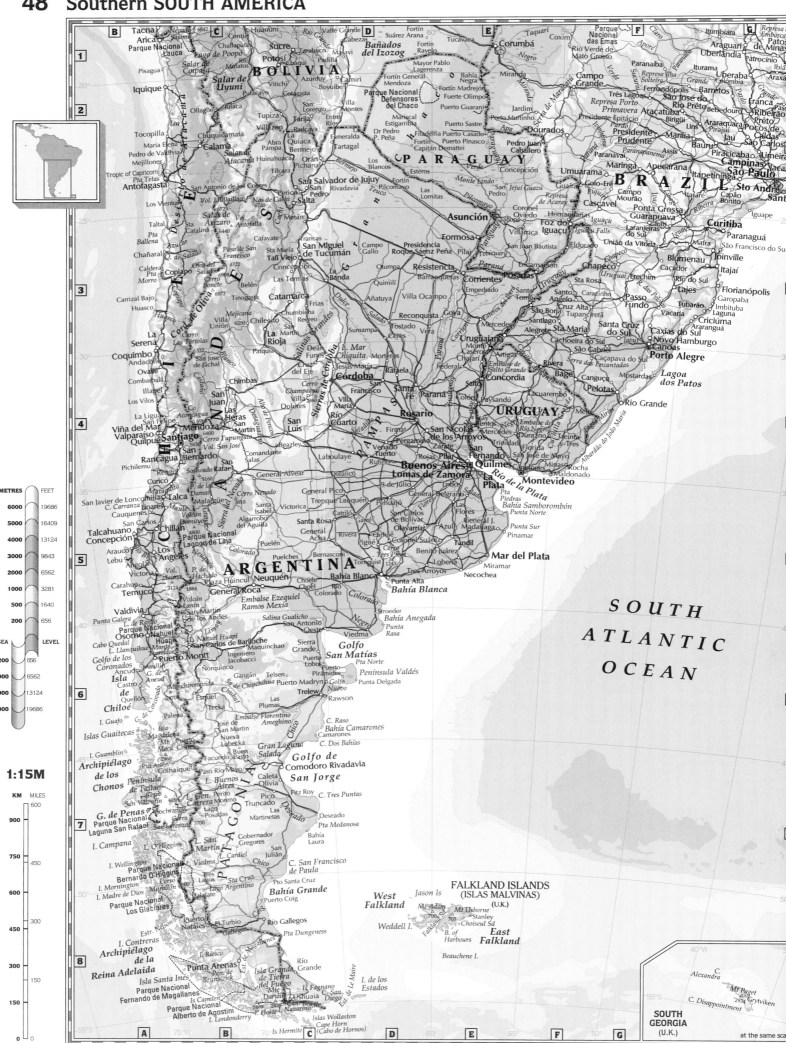

METRES   FEET
6000   19686
5000   16409
4000   13124
3000   9843
2000   6562
1000   3281
500   1640
200   656
SEA   LEVEL
200   656
2000   6562
4000   13124
6000   19686

1:15M

KM   MILES
         600
900
         450
750
         300
600
         150
300
         0

Lambert Azimuthal Equal Area Projection

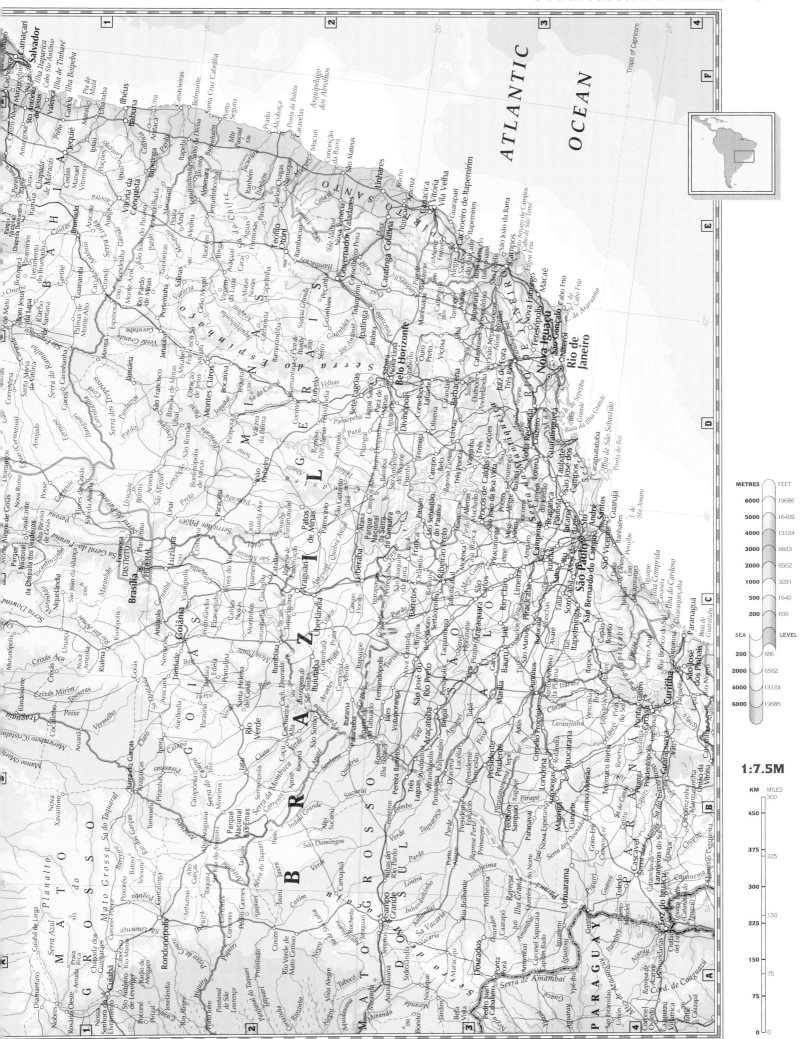

ATLANTIC

OCEAN

Tropic of Capricorn

METRES   FEET
6000   19686
5000   16409
4000   13124
3000   9843
2000   6562
1000   3281
500   1640
200   656
SEA   LEVEL
200   656
2000   6562
4000   13124
6000   19686

1:7.5M

KM   MILES
            300
450
            225
375
300   150
225
            75
150

75

0   0

© Collins

Lambert Azimuthal Equal Area Projection

METRES / FEET
METRES	FEET
6000	19686
5000	16409
4000	13124
3000	9843
2000	6562
1000	3281
500	1640
200	656
SEA	LEVEL
200	656
2000	6562
4000	13124
6000	19686

CAPE VERDE

at the same scale

Lambert Azimuthal Equal Area Projection

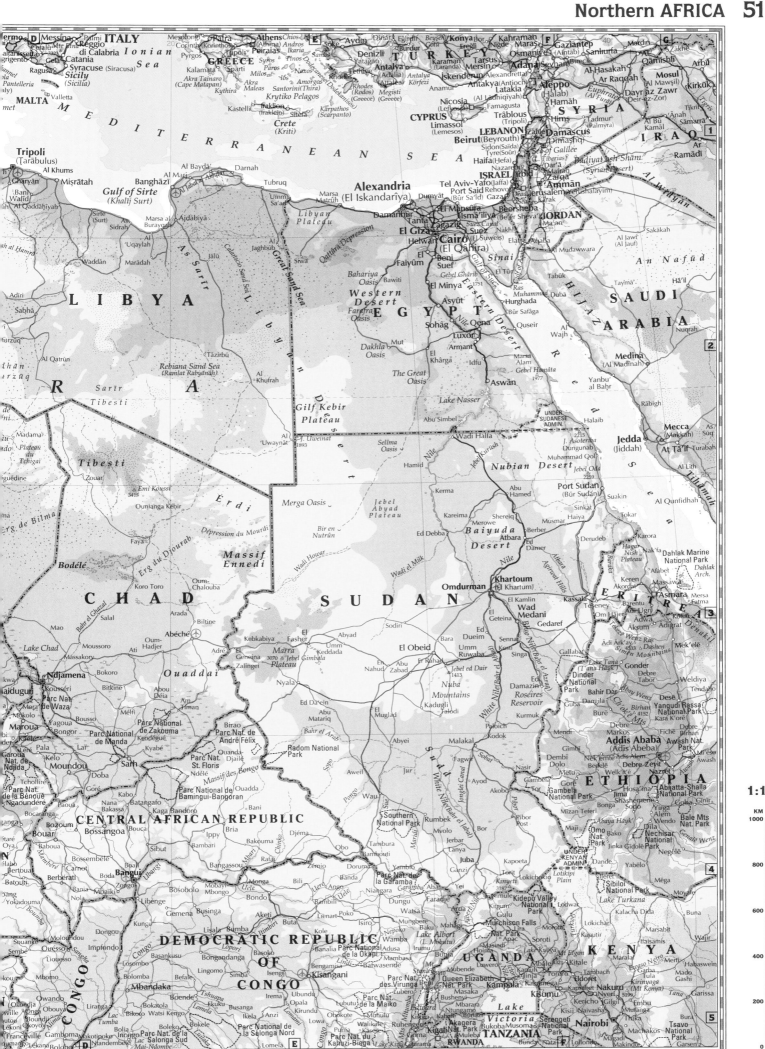
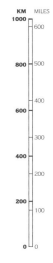

1:16M

KM MILES
© Collins

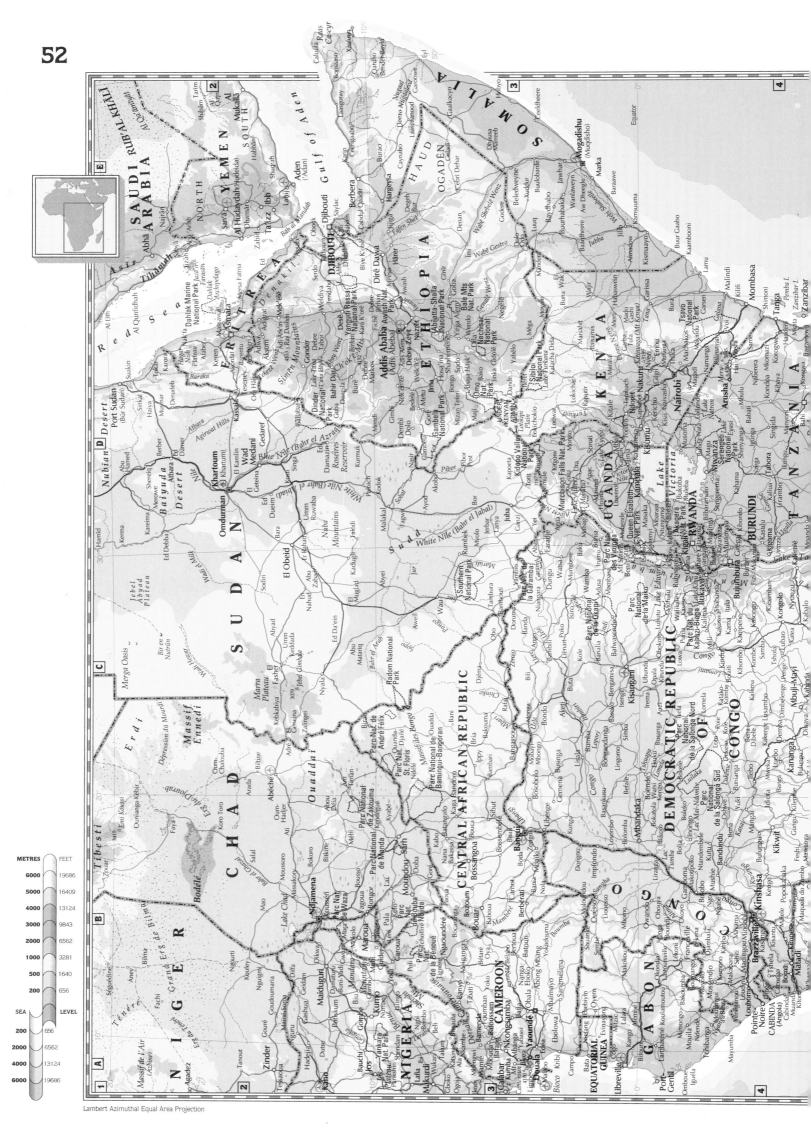

1:16M

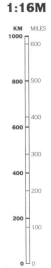

© Collins

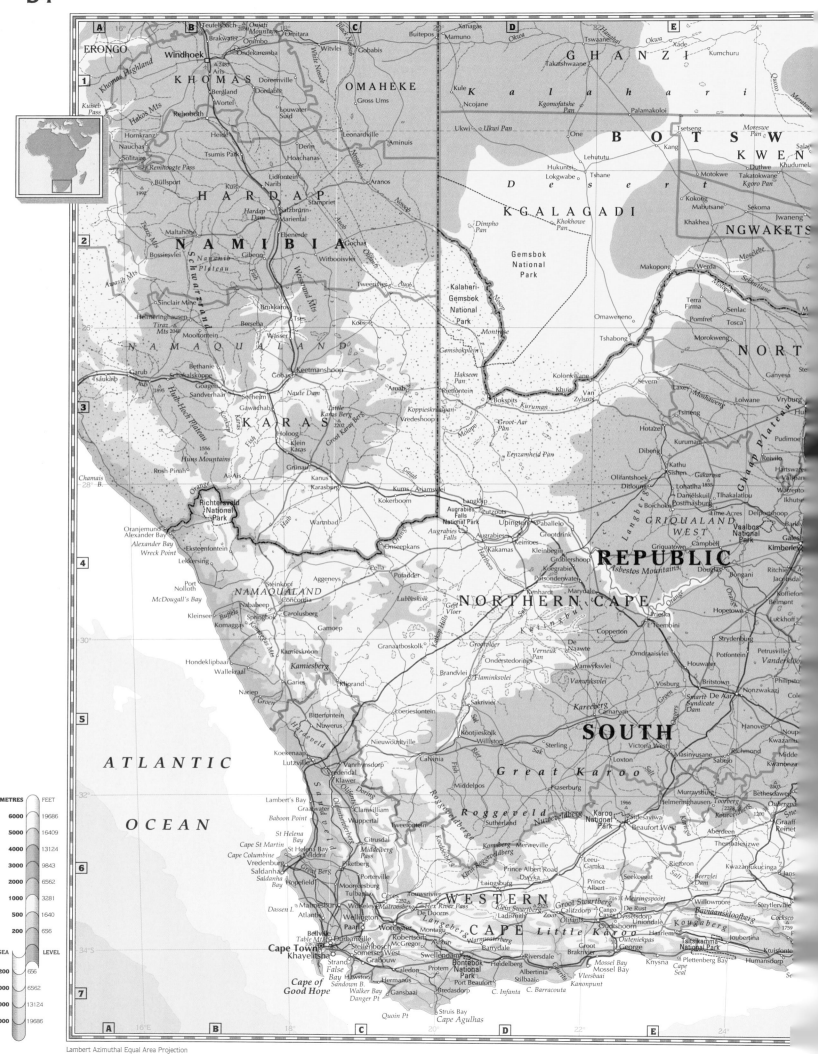

Lambert Azimuthal Equal Area Projection